THE SPACE BETWEEN

HYLA ARCHITECTS

ORO EDITIONS

Publishers of Architecture, Art, and Design
Gordon Goff: Publisher

www.oroeditions.com
info@oroeditions.com

Published by ORO Editions

www.hyla.com.sg
admin@hyla.com.sg
IG: hyla_architects
FB: hyla.architects

Graphic Design: MAKE Design
Text: Luo Jingmei
ORO Editions Managing Editor: Kirby Anderson

10 9 8 7 6 5 4 3 2 1 First Edition

Library of Congress data available upon request.
World Rights: Available

ISBN: 978-1-957183-17-6

Color Separations and Printing: ORO Editions, Inc.
Printed in China.

International Distribution:
www.oroeditions.com/distribution

ORO Editions makes a continuous effort to minimize the overall carbon footprint of its publications. As part of this goal, ORO Editions, in association with Global ReLeaf, arranges to plant trees to replace those used in the manufacturing of the paper produced for its books. Global ReLeaf is an international campaign run by American Forests, one of the world's oldest nonprofit conservation organizations. Global ReLeaf is American Forests' education and action program that helps individuals, organizations, agencies, and corporations improve the local and global environment by planting and caring for trees.

THE SPACE BETWEEN

HYLA ARCHITECTS

ORO
EDITIONS
NOVATO, CALIFORNIA

FOREWORD

By Luo Jingmei

"Architecture is about how one designs the spaces between the user and the environment. Just that one sentence defines everything that I believe in and do about architecture."
——— Han Loke Kwang

In the 29 years that Han Loke Kwang has led HYLA Architects, he has amassed a strong body of work that exhibits rigour and sensitivity to tropical house design. The expressions are modern, employing an architectural language of clarity, simplicity, honesty and dynamism. There is also a strong desire to create liveable, comfortable and enriching spaces, which put the users at the centre of the architecture. The way he does this is by addressing the particularities of living in Singapore, with its distinctive climate conditions of heat, glare and perennial rainfall, as well as challenges of urban density. How to react to such situations has become a sort of on-going thesis for the firm, using the single-family dwelling as the main vehicle for experimentation.

This book offers 25 unique house designs as a follow up to the firm's first monograph. The diversity showcases the firm's constant reinvention of house design in Singapore, particularly of the semi-detached and intermediate terrace variety. For Han, the house typology offers the widest scope of creative inspiration, devoid of the profit-driven and impersonal nature of large, commercial projects.

> "When I design houses, it is a very particular design for a particular family at a particular site at a particular moment. To me, that is a more interesting problem."

Over the years, the firm has sought different expressions with which to uncover new solutions. Many times, it is through reinterpreting the building skin by modulating its texture, materiality, depth and form. Concrete House is one example, with a concrete brise-soleil that provides shade and privacy for the inhabitants; at times, it becomes spatial, turning from mere skin into a semi-outdoor space where tropical living can be easily enjoyed. Another common strategy is the treatment of the building envelope with tectonic ingenuity, such as House Without Roof, which is a fitting representative as the book cover's image. Here, the archetypal house form with a pitched roof extends over internal and external spaces to blur the definition of thresholds and rooms.

Han has coined the phrase The Space Between to his approach. This 'space' refers to the physical space between the users and their environment. Shaping the architecture alters the relationship between the inhabitants and their environment – what and who is outside, the climate, the views, the social connections, etc. The perceptions are also aesthetic. Han's belief in architecture as the eminent art form grounds his desire for creating spaces that not only work well but are also beautiful for people to enjoy and to be in.

> "Forms be still, but spaces flow."

But unlike other art forms, architecture embodies function and is built to last for a time. The strong and stable forms in Han's buildings exhibit this permanence. Concrete, stone and brick form the backbone of many of his houses, accentuating this feeling of stability and protection. Within these shells, however, there is lightness and fluidity in the organisation.

> "I like my spaces to be dynamic, to flow so that people will have a sense of what is outside the immediate space, where they can go next and not feel trapped in the space."

This flow also refers to the connections between internal and external spaces. In plan and section, boundaries are dematerialised. Many rooms open to courtyards, patios and landscaped spaces such that when one is indoors, one also feels a part of the outdoors. Likewise, when one is outside, there is the feeling of being somewhat inside through manipulations of sheltering elements.

> "We don't have a physical style, but a philosophical style."

While each output is so different, the houses are bounded by a common adherence to five core values: honesty, simplicity, clarity, strength and dynamism. The last represents Han's restless spirit – restlessness for innovation, irreverence, and an unending search for beauty and utility in his work.

Room Without Roof

The firm's persistent search for new ways to create homes that work passively with the regional climate has resulted in some inventive appropriation of recognisable tropes. This two-storey brick structure is one of them. It has the archetypal form of a gable-roofed house but with a twist – part of the envelope shelters an external courtyard with a swimming pool. Above it, the roof opens up into a trellis that lets wind penetrate but also provides a substantial amount of shade in the daytime.

Because of this gesture, a typically external part of the house is internalised or, as the firm describes it, becomes 'a room without a roof'. Is it indoors or out? The threshold becomes blurred. This ambiguity is underscored by the extension of the roof over the attic, which reads as a vertical extension of the courtyard with its semi-openness and strip of landscaping.

By nature of the walls that shelter the courtyard, public views are controlled both ways. A strategy of screening – for both privacy and shade – underpins the choice and treatment of materials, which lend a decorative effect to the house's large planes. The external walls' dark grey face brick is modulated either with brick-sized openings or protruding bricks. Along the longitudinal wall of the second storey facing the pool, a large surface of precast concrete breezeblocks extends upward to form the attic's parapet. The last element in the external palette is a gridded timber screen that offers a warm contrast to the dominant application of brick and concrete while adding to the permeability of the home.

Project Name
— Room Without Roof
Type
— New build of two-storey detached house with an attic and a swimming pool
Location
— Siglap Plain, Singapore
Completed
— 2017
Built area
— 720m^2
Site area
— 558m^2
Project team members
— Han Loke Kwang
— Kompiya Rattanangkul
— Goh Chiou Hwa
Structural Engineer
— GNG Consultants Pte Ltd
Main Contractor
— V-Tech Construction Pte Ltd
Photography
— Derek Swalwell

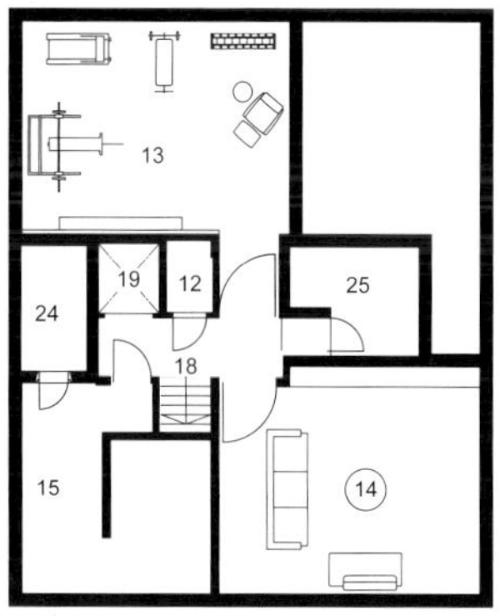

BASEMENT

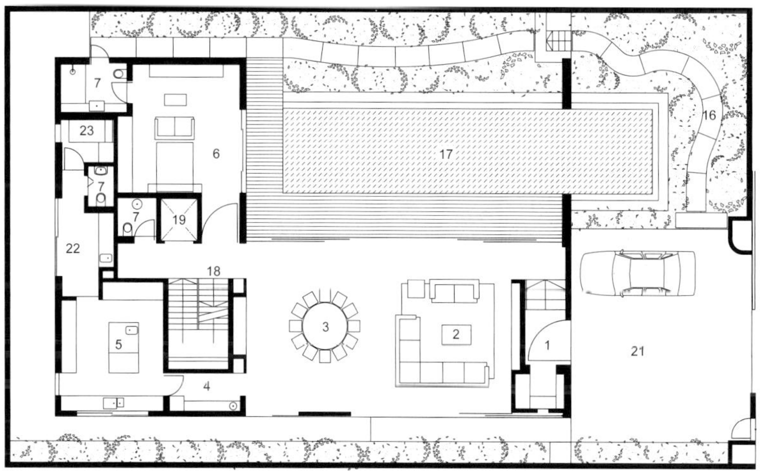

1ST STOREY

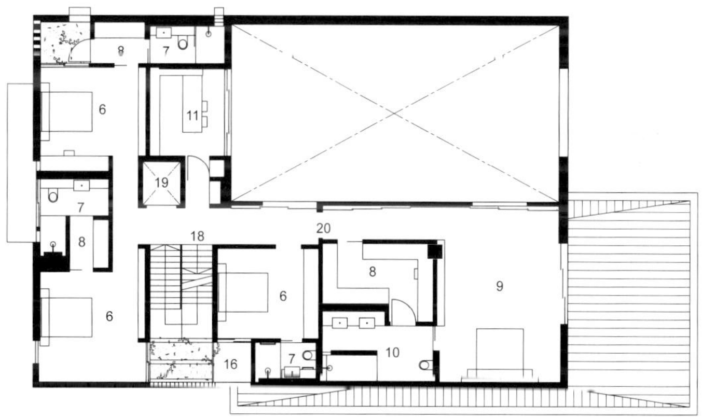

2ND STOREY

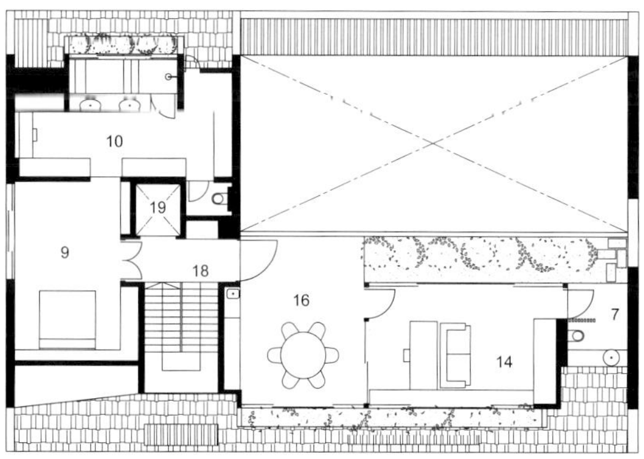

ATTIC

1 FOYER
2 LIVING
3 DINING
4 PANTRY
5 KITCHEN
6 BEDROOM
7 BATHROOM
8 WARDROBE
9 MASTER BEDROOM
10 MASTER BATHROOM
11 STUDY
12 WINE CELLAR
13 GYM
14 ENTERTAINMENT ROOM
15 STORE
16 TERRACE
17 POOL
18 STAIRS
19 LIFT
20 CORRIDOR
21 CAR PORCH
22 LAUNDRY
23 UTILITY
24 HOUSEHOLD SHELTER
25 M&E

Vertical Oasis

— The tectonic composition and vertical emphasis of this house conjure up imagery of natural landforms such as cliffs and rocky outcrop. On one side of the front façade are two stacked planes, textured with timber at the bottom and stone at the top. The only view into the house from the front elevation is through a large void between this composition of planes and a tall sidewall.

The void houses a koi pond, which melds with the swimming pool. The inward-looking architecture is a result of the house's location that looks directly out to an oncoming road. Like several of the firm's other houses, the strategy is to close up any connection to the street and create private sceneries on the interior. On the first storey, the double-storey living and dining areas open to the courtyard through full-height, slide-and-fold doors that can fully retract to link internal and external spaces. To accentuate the vertical quality of the house, the master bedroom is given a double-storey height. The expansiveness of the spaces lends the house a generous spirit.

A trellis made from glass and anodised aluminium protects the courtyard as well as the adjacent tall spaces from rain and glare. It combines with the ventilation provided by the large void at the front to create a thermally comfortable and private environment – a veritable oasis. Shadows thrown onto the large wall surface add to the conviviality and theatricality this courtyard offers.

Project Name
— Vertical Oasis
Type
— New build of two-storey semi-detached house with an attic and a swimming pool
Location
— Ripley Crescent, Singapore
Completed
— 2022
Built area
— 673m^2
Site area
— 446m^2
Project team members
— Han Loke Kwang
— Tran Thi Thu Trang
— Nicholas Teoh
Structural Engineer
— ASE Consultants
Main Contractor
— Emma Groups Construction Pte Ltd
Photography
— Derek Swalwell

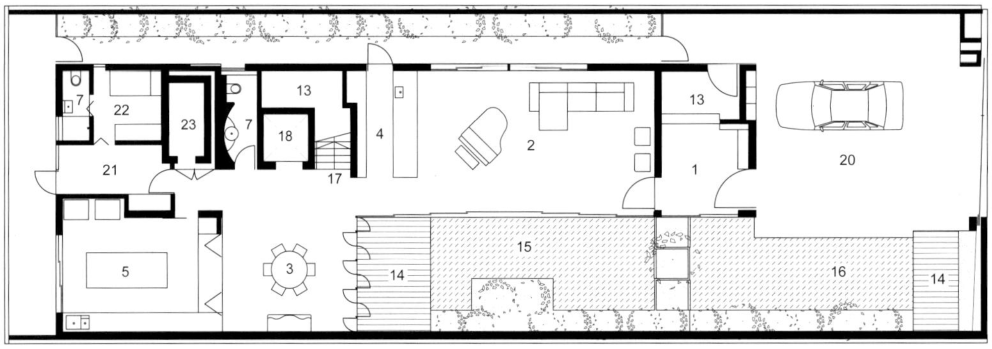

1ST STOREY

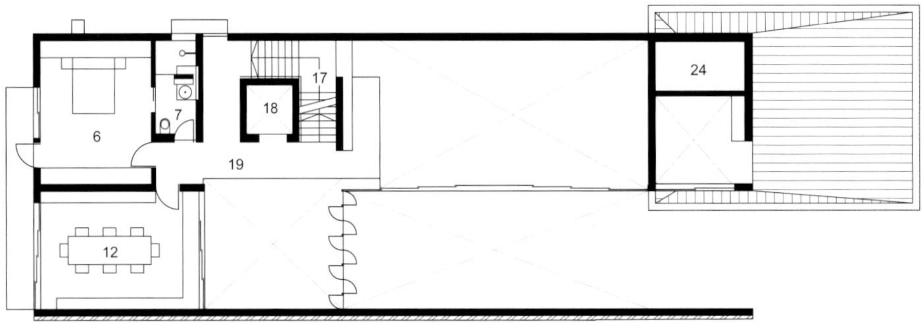

MEZZANINE

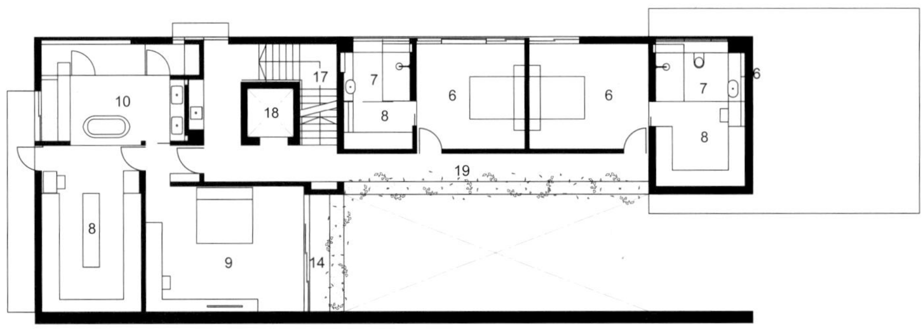

2ND STOREY

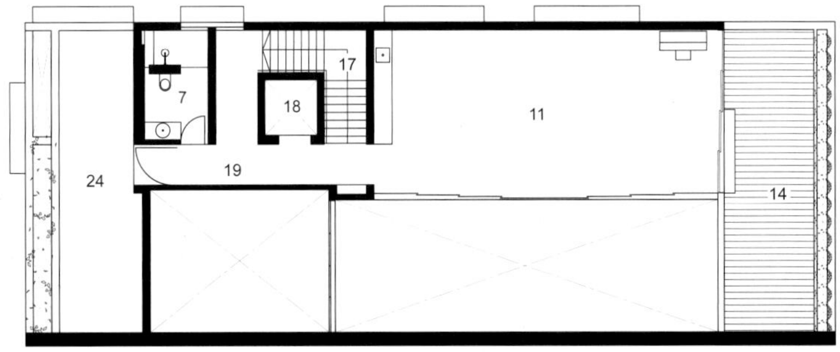

ATTIC

1 FOYER
2 LIVING
3 DINING
4 BAR
5 WET KITCHEN
6 BEDROOM
7 BATHROOM
8 WARDROBE
9 MASTER BEDROOM
10 MASTER BATHROOM
11 FAMILY ROOM
12 STUDY
13 STORE
14 TERRACE
15 KOI POND
16 POOL
17 STAIRS
18 LIFT
19 CORRIDOR
20 CAR PORCH
21 LAUNDRY
22 UTILITY
23 HOUSEHOLD SHELTER
24 M&E

Concrete Light

—— The pitched roof form is commonly deployed in this part of the world for its pragmatic ability to quickly dispel rainwater. Here, it becomes the vehicle for formal and material expression, birthing a house with a monolithic quality and raw tactility. A concrete roof covers the house and swimming pool, blurring indoors and outdoors, and roof and walls. It creates a triple-volume courtyard, around which the spaces are planned.

The protective character of this concrete shell is lightened by an array of apertures put together to form a lattice. The interior experience is animated by the framing of the apertures against the exterior green, which extends indoors at parts through gardens and planters to bring relief.

To give in-depth study to the geometry of the form, structural functionality, modularity and porosity, model making proved exceptionally useful. Vertical and horizontal balsa wood strips were cut to represent each concrete column and beam, as well as each modular louvre. This meticulous approach persisted in the construction. The individual concrete modules were based on the dimensions of the actual pine formwork. We expressed the difference in measurements of these modules from the structural requirements with a chamfer detail. The decision to highlight this disparity instead of hiding it enables the retention of the legibility of the module, which orders the planning of spaces and function. This brings to the project a refreshing rigour and consciousness.

Project Name
—— Concrete Light
Type
—— New build of two-storey semi-detached house with a basement, an attic and a swimming pool
Location
—— Greenleaf Drive, Singapore
Completed
—— 2018
Built area
—— 492m^2
Site area
—— 341m^2
Project team members
—— Han Loke Kwang
—— Tran Thi Thu Trang
Structural Engineer
—— Thymn Pte Ltd
Main Contractor
—— Emma Groups Construction Pte Ltd
Photography
—— Derek Swalwell

SME 3783Z

BASEMENT

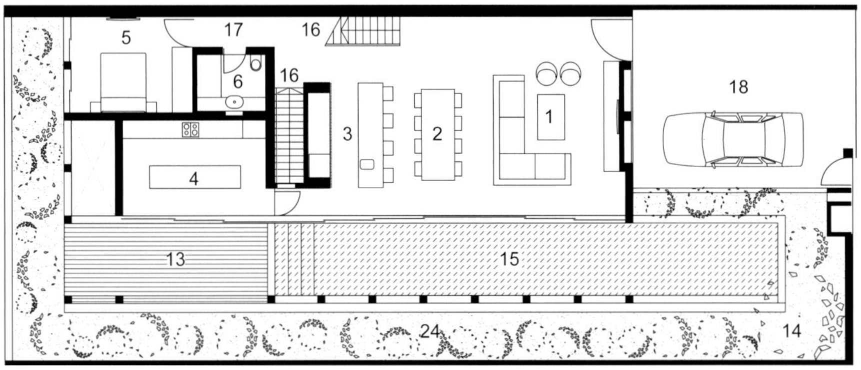

1ST STOREY

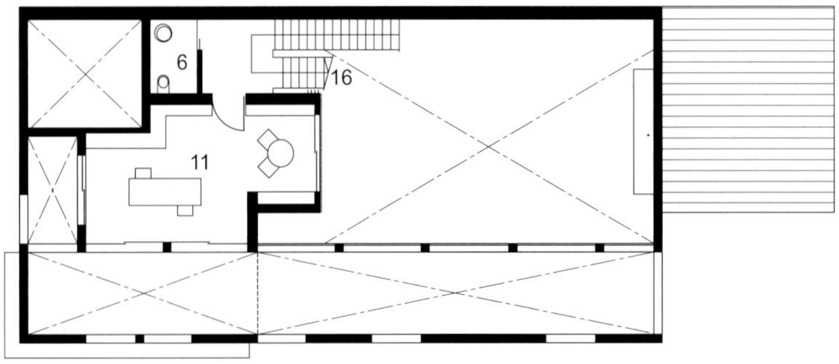

MEZZANINE

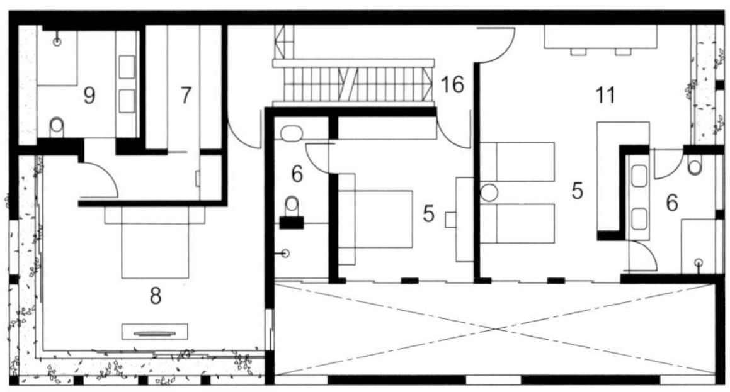

2ND STOREY

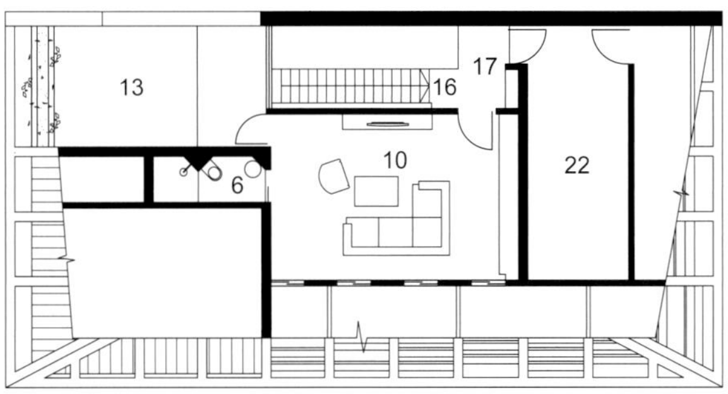

ATTIC

1 LIVING
2 DINING
3 DRY KITCHEN
4 WET KITCHEN
5 BEDROOM
6 BATHROOM
7 WARDROBE
8 MASTER BEDROOM
9 MASTER BATHROOM
10 FAMILY ROOM
11 STUDY
12 STORE
13 TERRACE
14 GARDEN
15 POOL
16 STAIRS
17 CORRIDOR
18 CAR PORCH
19 LAUNDRY
20 UTILITY
21 HOUSEHOLD SHELTER
22 M&E

Outside In

Designed for a family of five, the architecture of this house is highly contextual. It is sited on elevated ground, with the better view at the rear. Thus, the programmatic organisation was inverted, with the main living spaces, swimming pool and most bedrooms facing this superior vista. As the shape of the land tapers outward at the rear, this layout is optimal as it allows for more spacious gathering spaces.

A twelve-metre-high forecourt with a koi pond and a tall tree provides a pleasant introduction into the home. This buffer zone between public and private realms is indoors but feels a part of the external environment due to openings at the sidewall, and a light-filtering timber pergola and glass roof. A vocabulary of lines – lines of the ample brise-soleil and the shards of shadows that animate walls – defines this house. Horizontal timber slats cloak the front façade, placed closed enough for privacy. At the west-facing façade, a swivelling variation fronts the study room on the mezzanine, with each fin made from eight timber components.

This room, which cantilevers between the two party walls, functions as a deep overhang for the pool deck below and a buffer for the double-volume living and dining rooms. In order to stretch across the entire house's width sans columns, it is suspended from the top floor using a pair of deep beams that double as a planter for the master bedroom's verandah above. Throughout the house, many in-between spaces such as this add to its duality.

Project Name
— Outside In
Type
— New build of two-storey semi-detached house with an attic, a basement and a swimming pool
Location
— Watten View, Singapore
Completed
— 2021
Built area
— $778m^2$
Site area
— $450m^2$
Completed
— 2017
Project team members
— Han Loke Kwang
— Tran Thi Thu Trang
— Constans Tan
Structural Engineer
— GCE Consulting Engineers
Main Contractor
— Emma Groups Construction Pte Ltd
Photography
— Derek Swalwell

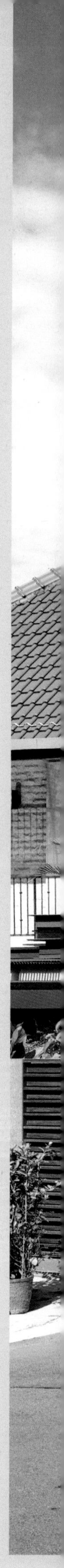

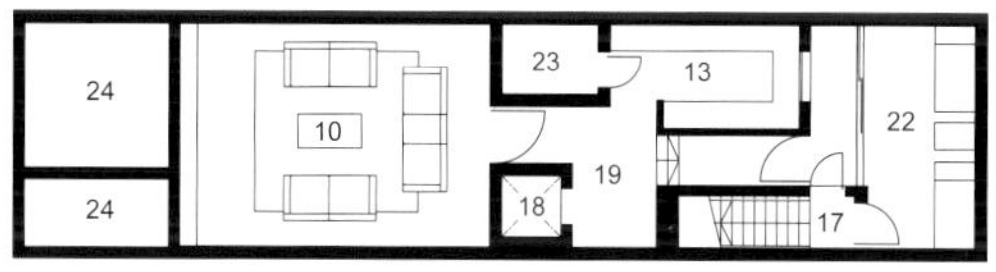

BASEMENT

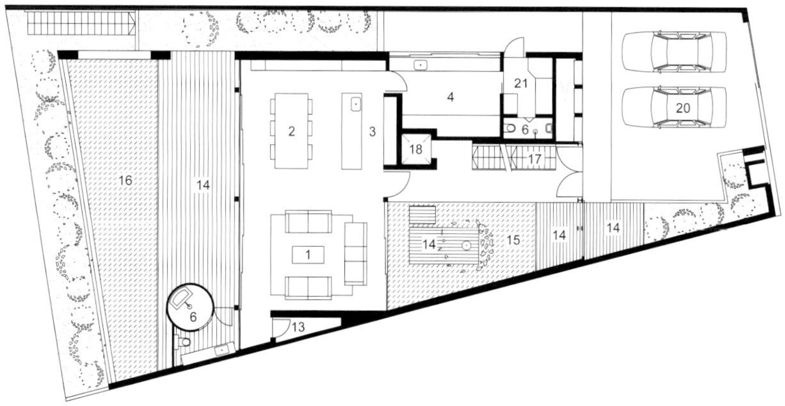

1ST STOREY

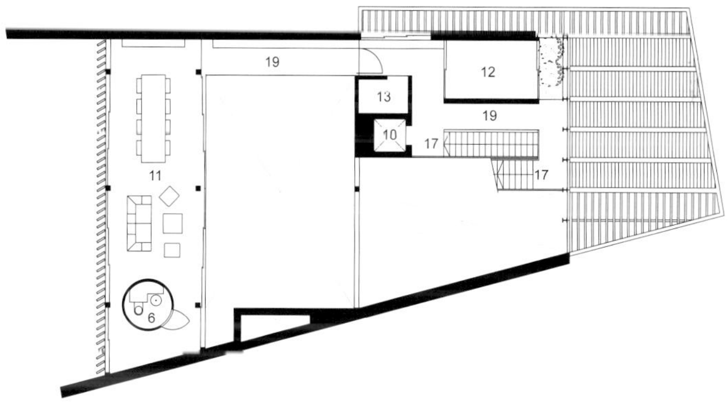

MEZZANINE

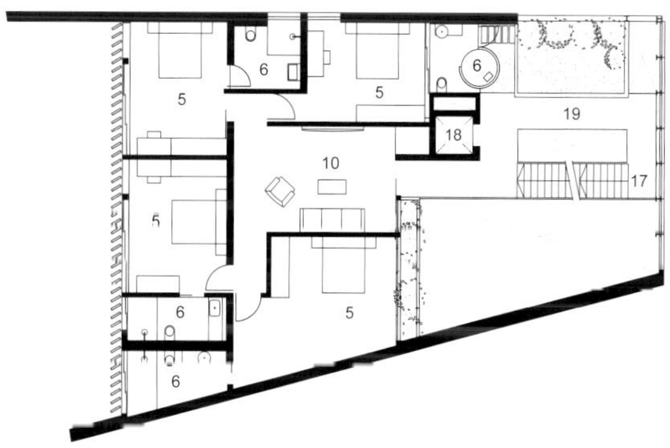

2ND STOREY

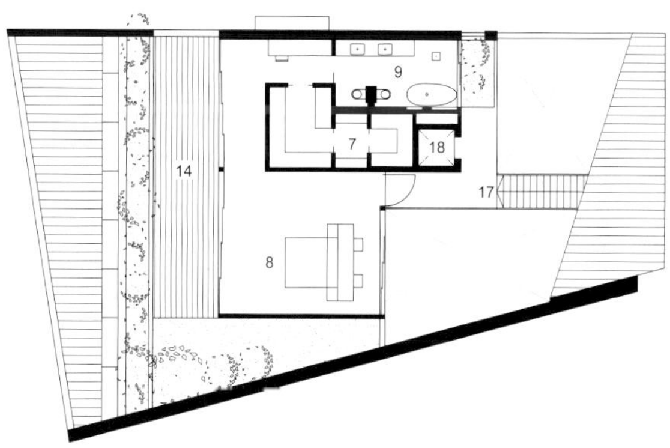

ATTIC

1 LIVING
2 DINING
3 DRY KITCHEN
4 WET KITCHEN
5 BEDROOM
6 BATHROOM
7 WARDROBE
8 MASTER BEDROOM
9 MASTER BATHROOM
10 FAMILY ROOM
11 STUDY
12 GYM
13 STORE
14 TERRACE
15 POND
16 POOL
17 STAIRS
18 LIFT
19 CORRIDOR
20 CAR PORCH
21 LAUNDRY
22 UTILITY
23 HOUSEHOLD SHELTER
24 M&E

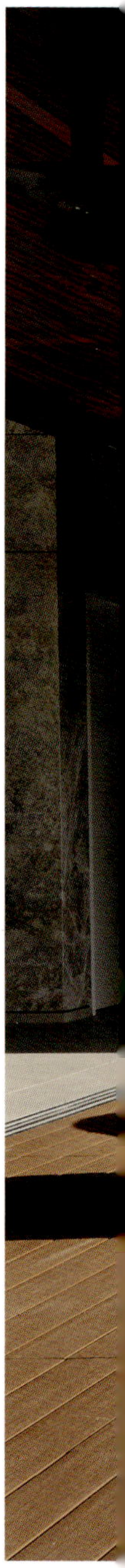

Custom Shades

— This modest corner terrace house continues the firm's exploration of the concrete screen. The use of concrete gives the house a strong tectonic quality, as opposed to the lightness of timber or metal screens. The screening language was a response to the context. The house needed to be blocked from a primary school at the side and its attendant noise and privacy issues, as well as sun exposure due to its east-west orientation.

The programmatic organisation relates to the unusual planning requirement of the house, which required larger setbacks at the rear to remain consistent with the existing street block. Thus, the kitchen is positioned at the front and the living room behind, fronted by a terrace. Three distinct strategies were conceived for each of the three elevations with regard to the views and orientation. An almost blank, off-form concrete wall at the side keeps out the view and noise from the school. At the front, a porous concrete screen lets in more natural light and ventilation. It encloses a balcony with lush planting that feasts on the morning sun.

At the rear, a screen of custom-made, pre-cast concrete blocks with smaller openings shields the main living room from the neighbour. The varied opening sizes give a playful, pixelated effect to the rear plane, which is further animated by glazing the openings with a combination of clear and stained glass. With the effect of sunlight, the delicate hues of pink and yellow soften yet add richness to the afternoon sun's rays, creating a glowing piece of art crafted from structure and skin.

Project Name
— Custom Shades
Type
— New build of two-storey corner terrace house with an attic
Location
— West Coast Grove, Singapore
Completed
— 2019
Built area
— 404m^2
Site area
— 239m^2
Project team members
— Han Loke Kwang
— Tiffany Ow
— Zoe Lim
— Kimberly Foo
Structural Engineer
— GCE Consulting Engineers
Main Contractor
— V-Tech Construction Pte Ltd
Photography
— Masano Kawana

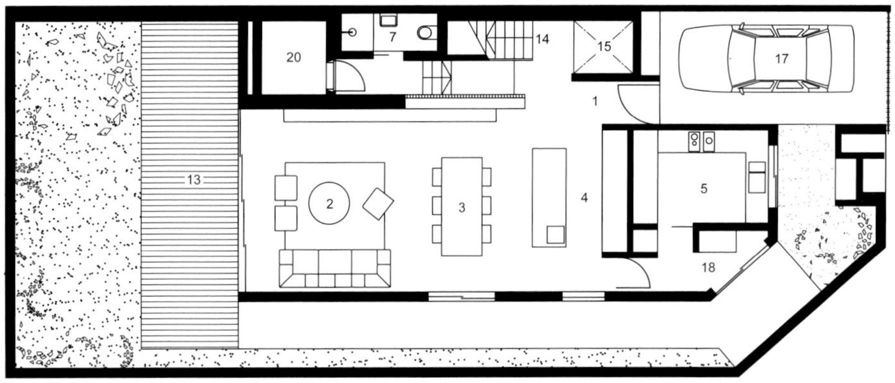

1ST STOREY

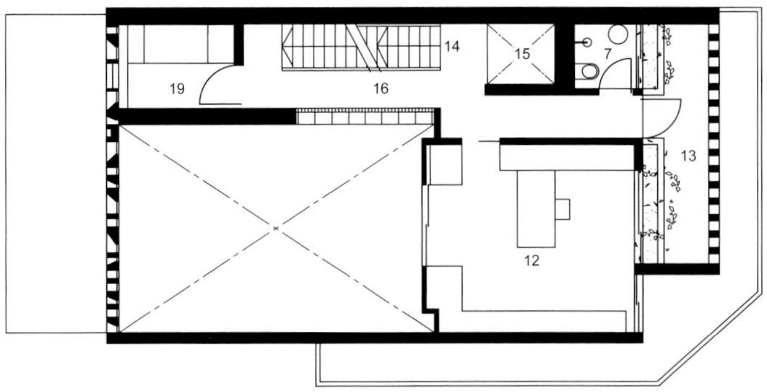

MEZZANINE

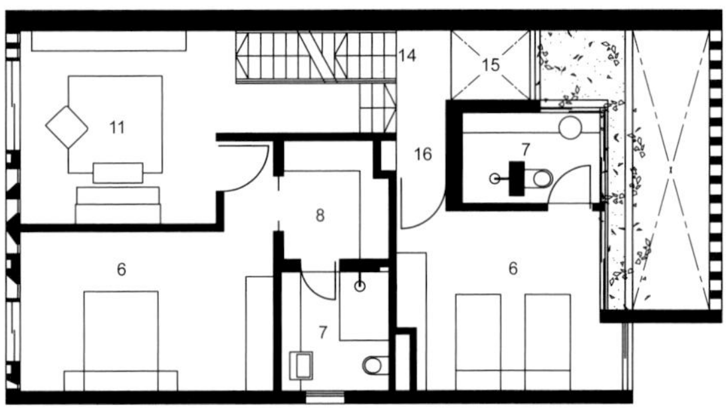

2ND STOREY

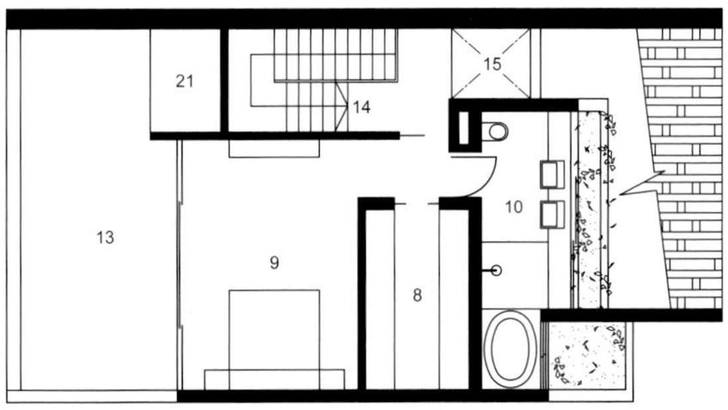

ATTIC

1 FOYER
2 LIVING
3 DINING
4 DRY KITCHEN
5 WET KITCHEN
6 BEDROOM
7 BATHROOM
8 WARDROBE
9 MASTER BEDROOM
10 MASTER BATHROOM
11 FAMILY ROOM
12 STUDY
13 TERRACE
14 STAIRS
15 LIFT
16 CORRIDOR
17 CAR PORCH
18 LAUNDRY
19 UTILITY
20 HOUSEHOLD SHELTER
21 M&E

Cascading Courts

Located on a long corner plot, the house's organisation is based alongside a series of cascading courts between the house and the party wall. This feature brings about a refreshing topographical way of moving through the home. The courtyards are roofed by a timber pergola and glass roof, which makes them essentially all-weather spaces. Ample greenery growing from deep planters and cross-breezes through large openings at the short elevations of the house bring relief to the interiors. Notably, the tiered arrangement of the courtyards makes them shady and usable spaces.

Lining up the rooms and common areas from front to back along the plot's length result in them being single-loaded spaces. Sandwiched between a wall of screened windows facing the street and the internal courtyards, they enjoy plenty of light and breeze. The architecture's clean mono-pitched form, as well as dense, vertical timber screens and off-form concrete walls produce an architectural shell with an almost Japanese simplicity. The raw materiality extends into the courtyard walls to make ambiguous the distinction between internal and external environments.

Full-height glazing on the first storey adds to the building's porosity. A bamboo garden outside these spaces enhances the tranquil mood. Several water features in the house reduce the ambient temperature. One is a cascading water feature at the entrance, backed by draping plants from a planter above. Abutting the double-storey family room on the second storey is another small pond, where a sole tree in the centre projects a meditative image against off-form concrete walls.

Project Name
— Cascading Courts
Type
— New build of two-storey semi-detached house with an attic
Location
— Faber Drive, Singapore
Completed
— 2017
Built area
— 568m^2
Site area
— 409m^2
Project team members
— Han Loke Kwang
— Navin Rungsmai
— Amanda Goh
Structural Engineer
— GNG Consultants Pte Ltd
Main Contractor
— Praxis Contractors Pte Ltd
Photography
— Derek Swalwell

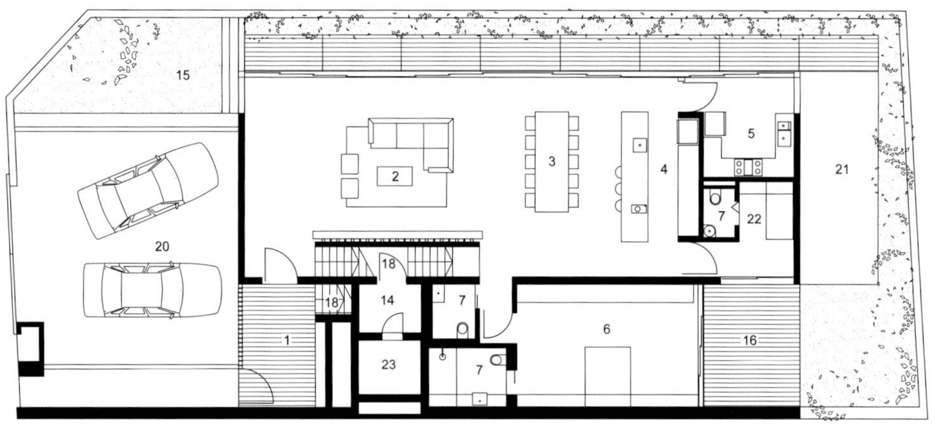

1ST STOREY

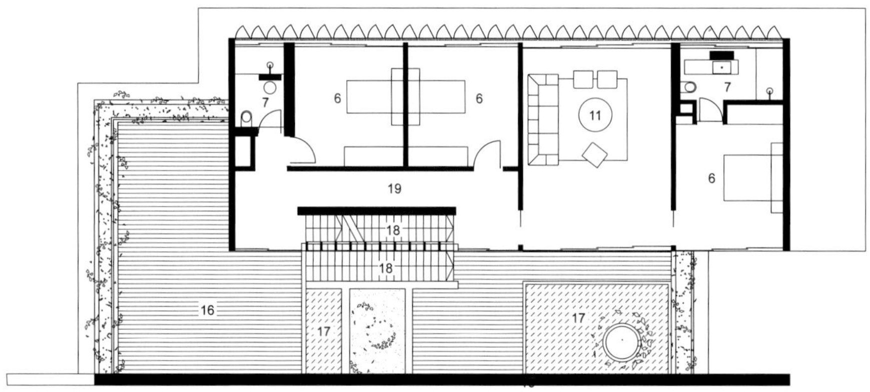

2ND STOREY

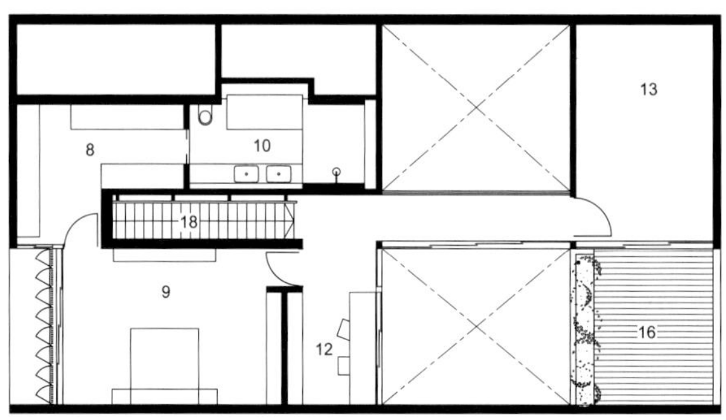

ATTIC

1 FOYER
2 LIVING
3 DINING
4 DRY KITCHEN
5 WET KITCHEN
6 BEDROOM
7 BATHROOM
8 WARDROBE
9 MASTER BEDROOM
10 MASTER BATHROOM
11 FAMILY ROOM
12 STUDY
13 MUSIC ROOM
14 STORE
15 GARDEN
16 TERRACE
17 FEATURE POND
18 STAIRS
19 CORRIDOR
20 CAR PORCH
21 LAUNDRY
22 UTILITY
23 HOUSEHOLD SHELTER

The Space Between Walls

In this house, the firm's use of courtyards to bring light, ventilation and private views into the semi-detached typology sees it disengaged not only from the party wall to create a linear void, but also from the front façade to shape an inviting water forecourt, the latter given privacy from the street with a tall wall made from blackened brick. The wall gives the exterior a reticent character, but behind it is an open living environment.

A layered, almost ritualistic sequence defines the access into the home. Firstly, the lush landscaping and calm still water at the forecourt demand pause. One then passes through a secondary portal in the form of a double-height timber wall that, like the brick façade, camouflages the door within its design. Inside the home, the water body expands into a lap pool that runs along the party wall, creating a tranquil oasis within the house. Along the pool, a timber pergola topped with glass washes comfortable light into the space.

The front elevation's brick materiality persists into the house as an infill between a gridded concrete structural frame. These materials' ruggedness accentuates a sense of the outdoors. A dogleg staircase that cantilevers over the pool is designed as a lightweight element for sunlight and wind to penetrate the gaps that replace risers. Upstairs, two more landscaped courtyards perpetuate the house's porosity. Despite the lack of an exterior view, the architecture manages to give its inhabitants the delight of being surrounded by gardens.

Project Name
— The Space Between Walls
Type
— New build of two-storey semi-detached house with an attic and a swimming pool
Location
— Princess of Wales Road, Singapore
Completed
— 2017
Built area
— 455m^2
Site area
— 350m^2
Project team members
— Han Loke Kwang
— Kompiya Rattanangkul
— Chong Wen Jin
Structural Engineer
— Thymn Pte Ltd
Main Contractor
— QS Builders Pte Ltd
Photography
— Derek Swalwell

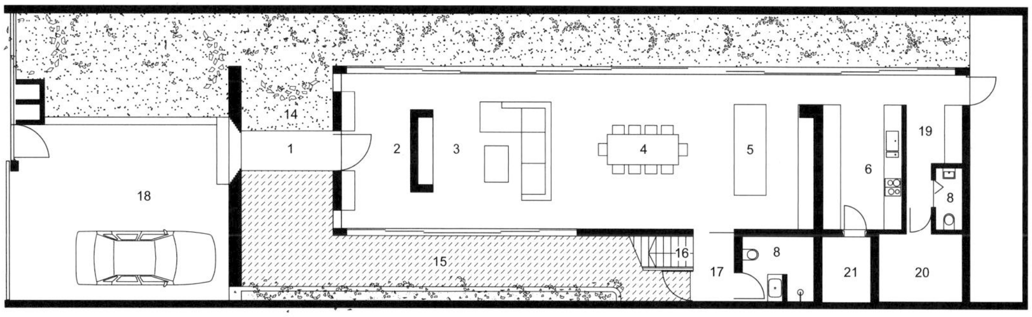

1ST STOREY

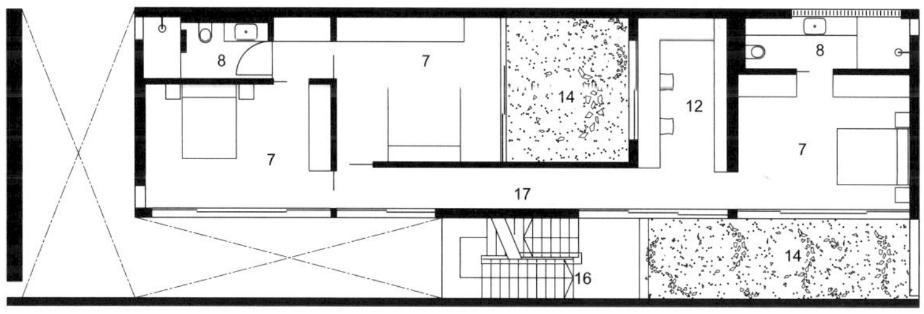

2ND STOREY

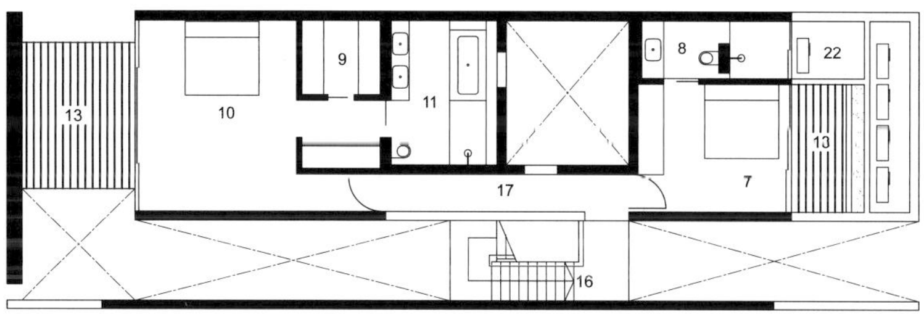

ATTIC

1 ENTRANCE
2 FOYER
3 LIVING
4 DINING
5 DRY KITCHEN
6 WET KITCHEN
7 BEDROOM
8 BATHROOM
9 WARDROBE
10 MASTER BEDROOM
11 MASTER BATHROOM
12 STUDY
13 TERRACE
14 COURTYARD
15 POOL
16 STAIRS
17 CORRIDOR
18 CAR PORCH
19 LAUNDRY
20 UTILITY
21 HOUSEHOLD SHELTER
22 M&E

SKU5913S

Viewing Back

Defined by a large granite wall, the front elevation of this two-storey brick house is unassuming and stoic. Yet, a rectangular cutout in the plane looking into greenery hints at a more enlivening internal experience. To introduce sunlight into the long and narrow plan, the house peels from the party wall, creating a linear courtyard. It terminates at the front façade with balconies, prompting physical enjoyment of the outdoors and a relationship to the street. Overlooking the stairwell, a study room enveloped in glass and three bedrooms participate in the delights of the courtyard.

In the house, attention is drawn upward with a staircase of floating treads rising up a three-storey atrium. A backdrop of landscaping perpetuates a tropical experience. At the rear elevation is a richer reward in the form of a panorama of the garden of Singapore's former Command House, which was built circa 1937 to 1938 as the official residence of the British General Officer Commanding (GOC) of Malaya and other military officials in 1971, and whose open grounds offer a breather in the dense residential neighbourhood.

To take advantage of this, the main spaces are placed at the rear and elevated to offer optimal vantage. An open plan that segues into a terrace and swimming pool allows unblocked vistas. A defining feature in the home is a sun-shading screen that turns downward at the pool to frame the view. When sunlight passes through its pattern of horizontal and vertical lines, the graphical shadows that is produced becomes a highlight.

Project Name
— Viewing Back
Type
— New build of two- storey semi-detached house with an attic and a swimming pool
Location
— Jalan Tempua, Singapore
Completed
— 2017
Built area
— 567m^2
Site area
— 403m^2
Project team members
— Han Loke Kwang
— Tran Thi Thu Trang
— Amanda Tay
— Wesley Fong
— Chong Wen Jin
Structural Engineer
— ACE Consulting Engineers
Main Contractor
— V-Tech Construction Pte Ltd
Photography
— Derek Swalwell

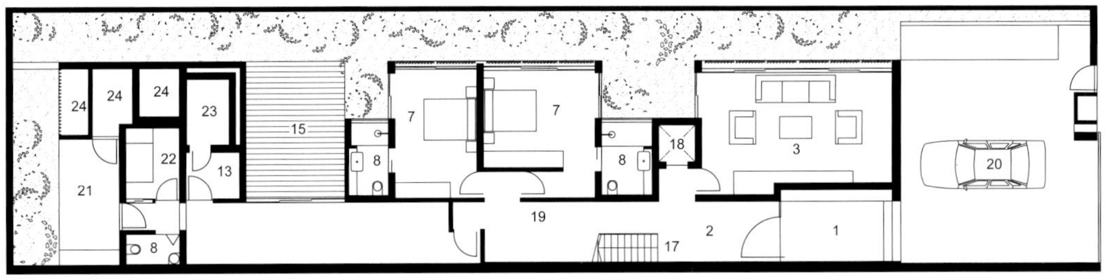

1ST STOREY

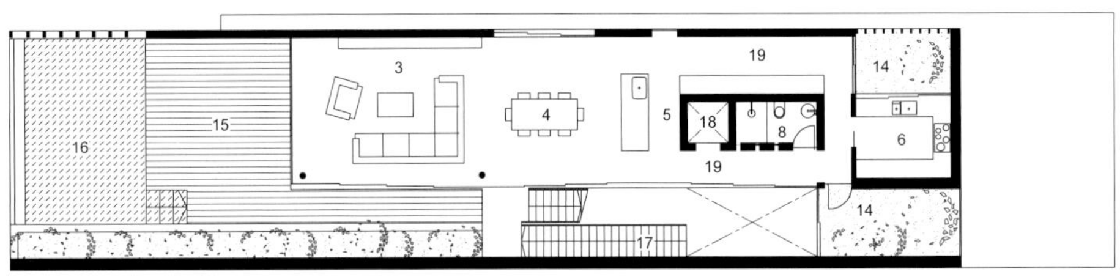

2ND STOREY

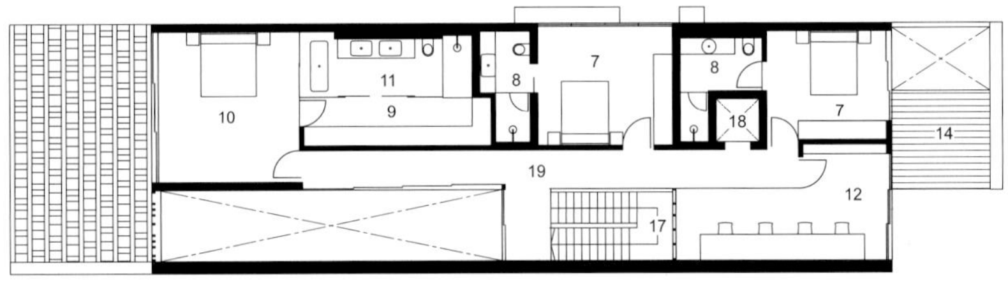

ATTIC

1 ENTRANCE
2 FOYER
3 LIVING
4 DINING
5 DRY KITCHEN
6 WET KITCHEN
7 BEDROOM
8 BATHROOM
9 WARDROBE
10 MASTER BEDROOM
11 MASTER BATHROOM
12 STUDY
13 STORE
14 COURTYARD
15 TERRACE
16 POOL
17 STAIRS
18 LIFT
19 CORRIDOR
20 CAR PORCH
21 LAUNDRY
22 UTILITY
23 HOUSEHOLD SHELTER
24 M&E

Surprising Seclusion

— This house's architecture is one of singularity and seclusion – singularity in form and materiality, and seclusion as a protective mechanism from the unfriendly context. Both the front and rear elevations face busy roads, and the southern end edges another house. The response is a simple form – a double-pitched volume that abstracts the local vernacular house – with its structural make up of a concrete frame and grey-faced brick-infill walls laid bare.

The architecture is at once familiar yet aloof, rudimentary yet abstract. Minimal openings in the shell give the house the character of a fortress. A counterpoint to the cavernous interior is a spacious courtyard with a reflective pool. This triple-volume atrium is the life force of the house, around which all the programs are organised. The staircase, with a base of sculpted treads and risers, cantilevers from a wall in this space toward the family room on the second storey. As it turns from the second storey to the attic, it takes on a more cloistered nature, accompanied by a stepped planter. Illumination from a skylight ensures a comfortable mix of lit and shadowed areas.

In the master bathroom, articulated brick walls exhibit consistency in the architecture. Gaps in the largely opaque planes allow for both ventilation and privacy. Both this space and the attic bathroom have planters that enliven the overall grey scheme. In the living, family and study room, custom storage units echo the architecture's geometric expressions in miniature.

Project Name
— Surprising Seclusion
Type
— New build of two- storey corner terrace house with an attic
Location
— Binchang Rise, Singapore
Completed
— 2017
Built area
— 360m²
Site area
— 298m²
Project team members
— Han Loke Kwang
— Chong Wen Jin
Structural Engineer
— GCE Consulting Engineers
Main Contractor
— Praxis Contractors Pte Ltd
Photography
— Derek Swalwell

60

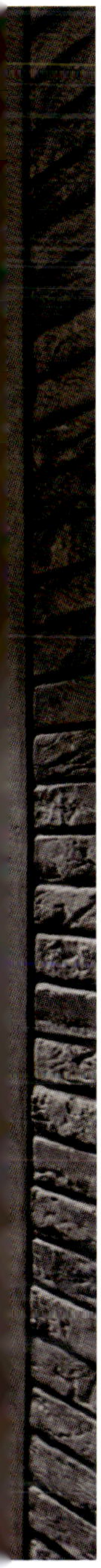

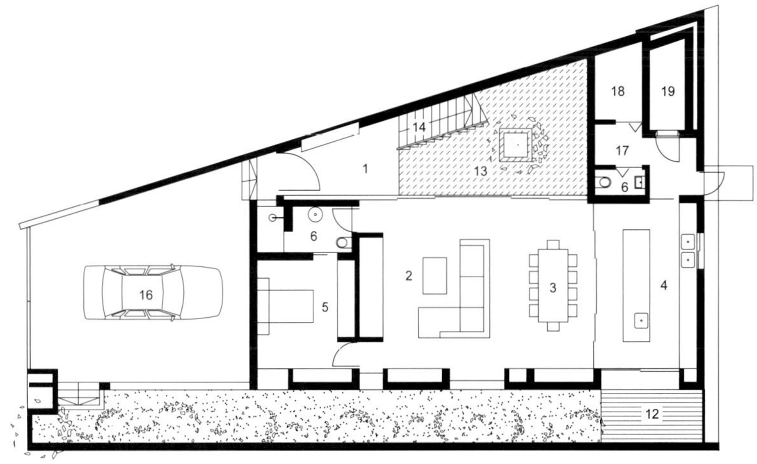

1ST STOREY

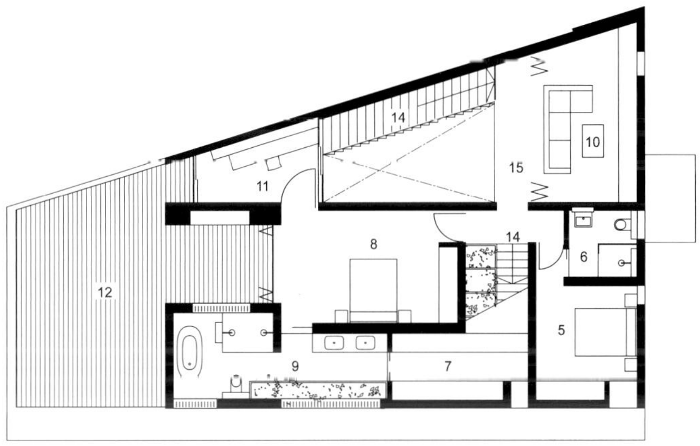

2ND STOREY

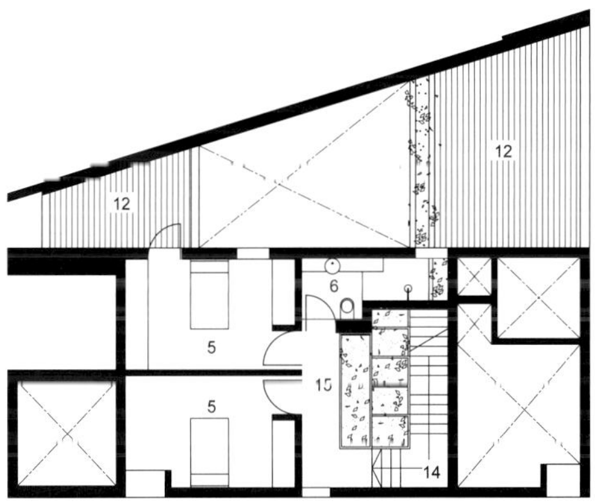

ATTIC

1 FOYER
2 LIVING
3 DINING
4 KITCHEN
5 BEDROOM
6 BATHROOM
7 WARDROBE
8 MASTER BEDROOM
9 MASTER BATHROOM
10 FAMILY ROOM
11 STUDY
12 TERRACE
13 WATER FEATURE
14 STAIRS
15 CORRIDOR
16 CAR PORCH
17 LAUNDRY
18 UTILITY
19 HOUSEHOLD SHELTER

Outside the Box

— Underpinning the unconventional façade of this house is an experimental response to building regulations. In Singapore, typical planning parameters place constraints on the house's envelope. It predetermines the forms seen on every street, which are governed by the same height, setback and slant of the attic line (that follows a maximum allowable roof pitch of 45 degrees from the attic floor). How far could the team push the boundaries of design while still complying with the rules?

At the front elevation, a big flat roof cantilevers from the attic line to disrupt the familiar domestic form while shielding the upper levels from the street. Below it, a secondary roof terrace breaks the façade into two overlapping rectangles, front to back. Next to the party wall, the cantilevering car porch roof continues the language of the main roof. The architecture eschews the firm's conventional response to the semi-detached typology that relies on courtyards to bring in light and breeze. Here, the large, glazed elevations do the same, with the long-span roofs protecting the interiors from heat and glare.

The magnanimity of the exterior forms is brought indoors with a double-volume living and dining room. The entertainment space on the mezzanine overlooks this area. Both are united with timber cladding juxtaposed against the facing brick of the party wall. A timber-clad wall on the lower level is both structure and furniture, with the television built into the custom storage. This warm materiality echoes on the house's side elevation, where a screen made from timber strips of different sizes lends interest to the vertical expanse.

Project Name
— Outside the Box
Type
— New build of two-storey semi-detached house with a mezzanine and an attic
Location
— Bloxhome Drive, Singapore
Completed
— 2020
Built area
— 421m²
Site area
— 260m²
Project team members
— Han Loke Kwang
— Tiffany Ow
— Na Hsi-en
Structural Engineer
— Thymn Pte Ltd
Main Contractor
— Emma Groups Construction Pte Ltd
Photography
— Daniel Koh

5

5

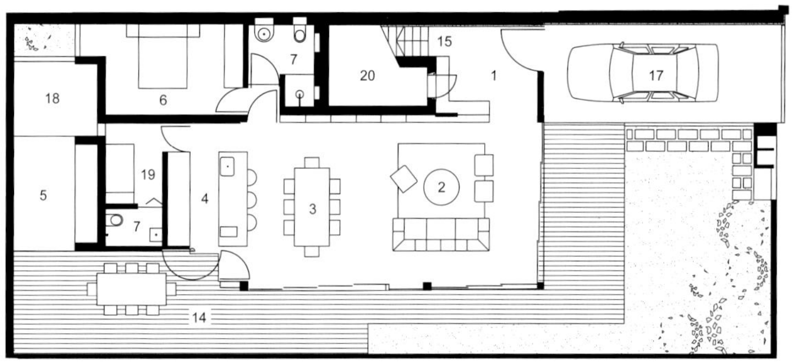

1ST STOREY

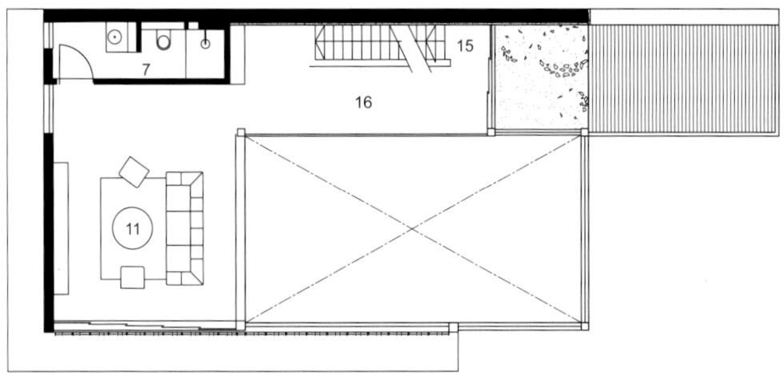

MEZZANINE

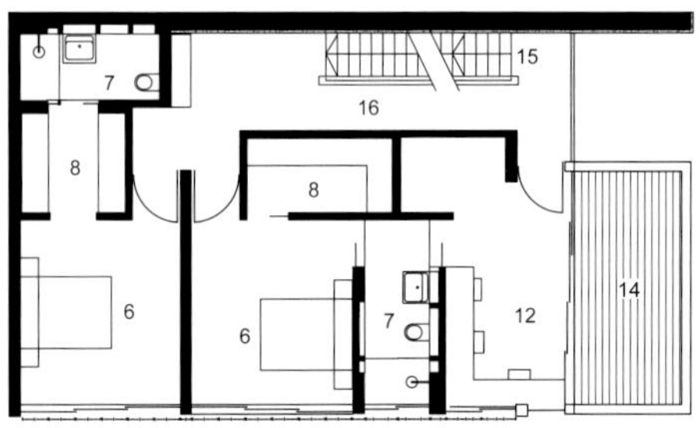

2ND STOREY

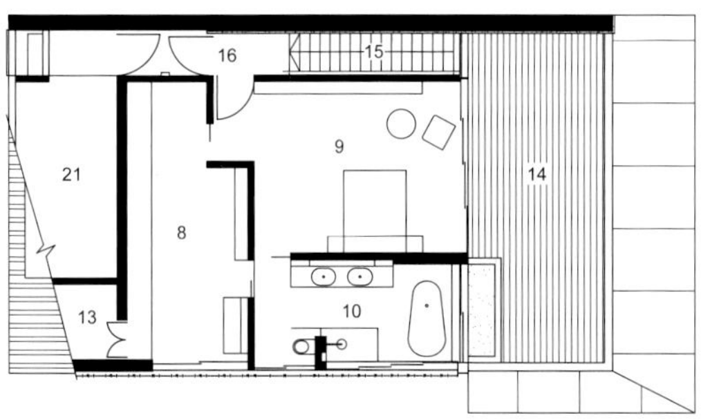

ATTIC

1 FOYER
2 LIVING
3 DINING
4 DRY KITCHEN
5 WET KITCHEN
6 BEDROOM
7 BATHROOM
8 WARDROBE
9 MASTER BEDROOM
10 MASTER BATHROOM
11 ENTERTAINMENT ROOM
12 STUDY
13 STORE
14 TERRACE
15 STAIRS
16 CORRIDOR
17 CAR PORCH
18 LAUNDRY
19 UTILITY
20 HOUSEHOLD SHELTER
21 M&E

Openly Screened

— Small plots add to the challenge of designing in the tropics, as inserting large courtyards is out of the question. Yet, this project is refreshing in its simplicity and brevity due to the employment of a pared-back approach in order to fit a loaded program into a mere 245-square-metre plot.

The first move was to tuck the utility areas into a small basement. This released the first storey for an open-plan living and dining, a dry and wet kitchen, a lift and even a fifteen-metre-long lap pool. The orthogonal massing is elementary and honest. An off-form concrete wall shields the front façade from the western sun and prying eyes. Despite this, the interior feels open and spacious. Glass doors on the first storey open up all three elevations to the outdoors. On the second storey, a sliver of timber screens on the front elevation interrupts the architecture's monolithic character, bringing light and breeze into the bedrooms.

The off-form concrete wall extends to the attic to hide a garden from street view. Screens filter light and views between the study and garden. This, as well as other small pockets of greenery, such as a courtyard that provides a view for the staircase, immerses the small house in its larger external environment. Whimsical gestures such as the sectional tapering of the staircase add to the delights found in this small home.

Project Name
— Openly Screened
Type
— New build of two-storey semi-detached house with a basement, an attic and a swimming pool
Location
— Chiselhurst Grove, Singapore
Completed
— 2017
Built area
— 374m^2
Site area
— 254m^2
Project team members
— Han Loke Kwang
— Chong Wen Jin
Structural Engineer
— NCL Consultants
Main Contractor
— iBuilders Pte Ltd
Photography
— Derek Swalwell

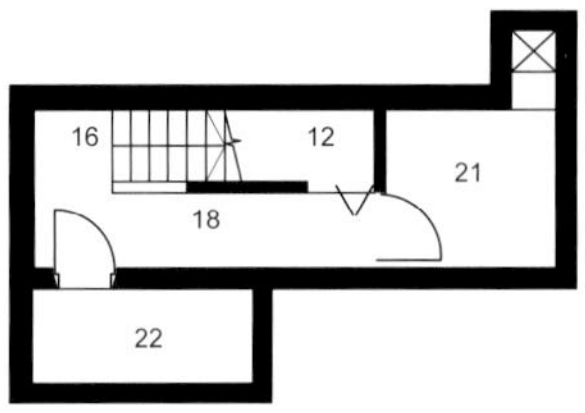

BASEMENT

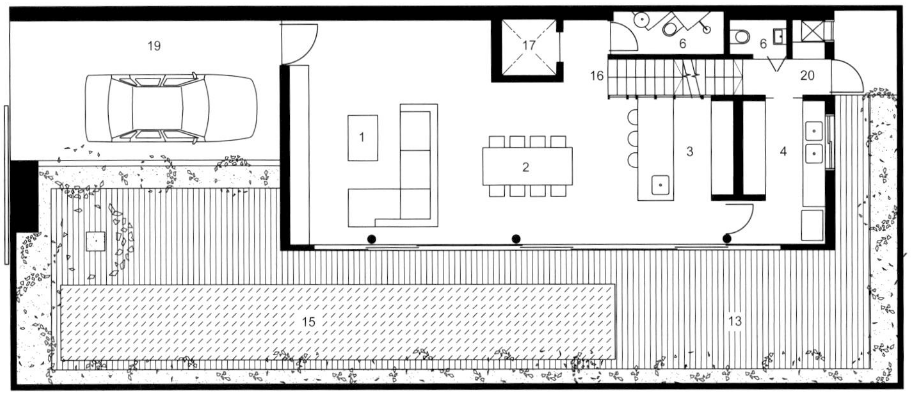

1ST STOREY

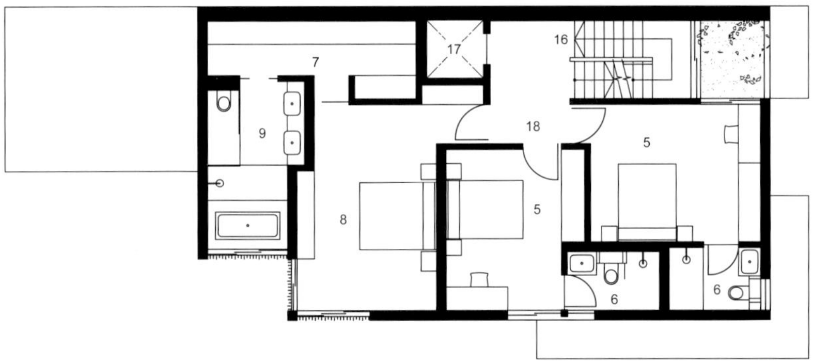

2ND STOREY

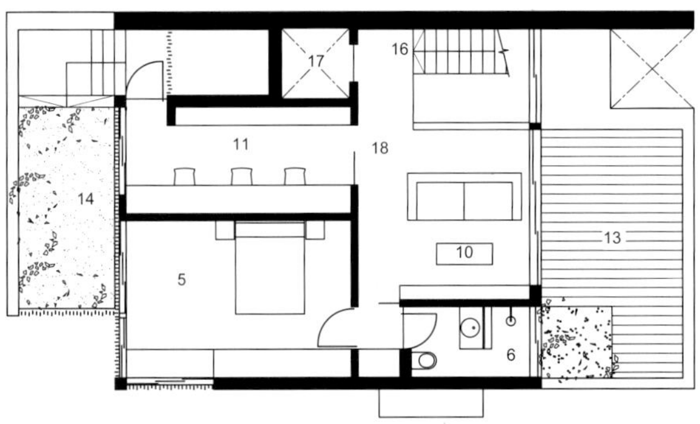

ATTIC

1 LIVING
2 DINING
3 DRY KITCHEN
4 WET KITCHEN
5 BEDROOM
6 BATHROOM
7 WARDROBE
8 MASTER BEDROOM
9 MASTER BATHROOM
10 FAMILY ROOM
11 STUDY
12 STORE
13 TERRACE
14 GARDEN
15 POOL
16 STAIRS
17 LIFT
18 CORRIDOR
19 CAR PORCH
20 LAUNDRY
21 UTILITY
22 HOUSEHOLD SHELTER

Higher Plane

The first impression of this house is not of a singular massing, but of horizontal volumes projecting outward to the street. The architectural push and pull in both the elevation and section was a response to the context of the site, which faces a public park with matured trees. The design challenge was how to relate to this situation: on the one hand, the greenery offers a good view, but on the other, there was the need for privacy.

The firm's answer was to raise the main living areas to the second storey. The swimming pool followed suit, becoming the intermediate space between the park and the house. The forty five-metre-deep plot allowed for this luxury. The living and dining, being elevated and set back from the front of the house, have complete privacy while enjoying the view of tree canopies. A large, operable gridded timber screen keeps the western sun out of these lofty spaces. The warm materiality extends to the cladding of the pool deck, the main gate, as well as the balcony of the master bedroom above. It is a choice decision, its naturalness merging the house with its verdant surroundings.

Along the party wall, a pair of steel-and-glass canopies provide shelter and shade to the circulation spaces and pool terrace. This brings natural light right down to the foyer on the first storey, where planters rising in tandem with the staircase introduces greenery deep into the plan. Apertures in the elevation along this trajectory augment the porosity of the home.

Project Name
— Higher Plane
Type
— New build of 2 storey semi-detached house with a mezzanine, an attic and a swimming pool
Location
— Greenfield Drive, Singapore
Completed
— 2021
Built area
— 722m^2
Site area
— 488m^2
Project team members
— Han Loke Kwang
— Nicholas Gomes
— Ulrich Chia
Structural Engineer
— GCE Consulting Engineers
Main Contractor
— Emma Groups Construction Pte Ltd
Photography
— Derek Swalwell

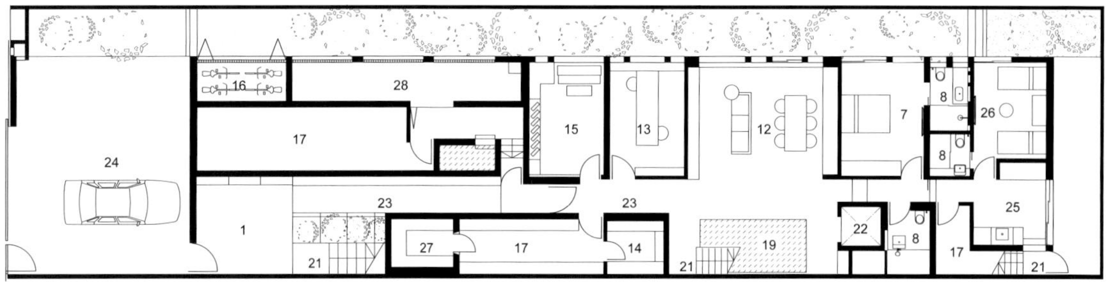

1ST STOREY

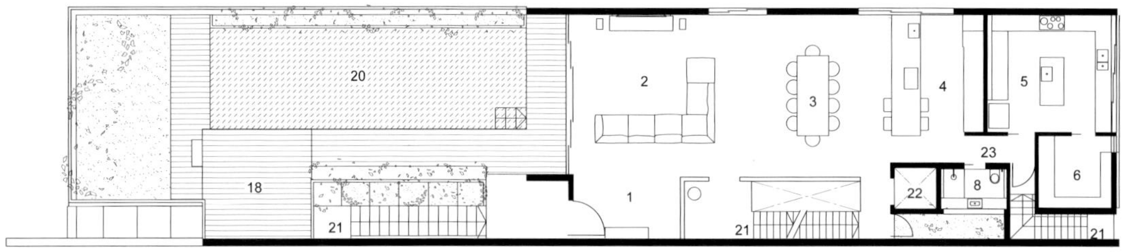

2ND STOREY

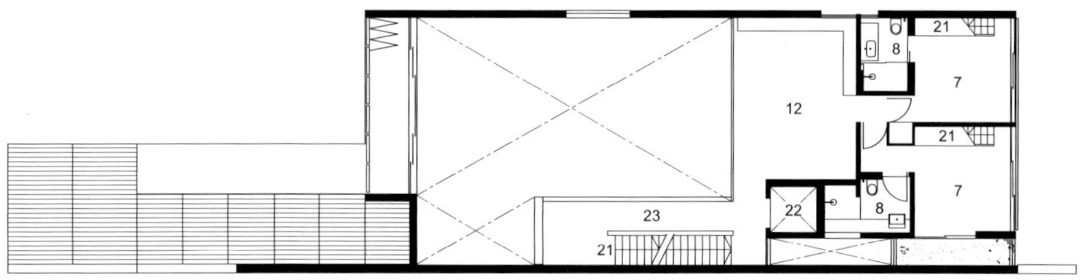

MEZZANINE

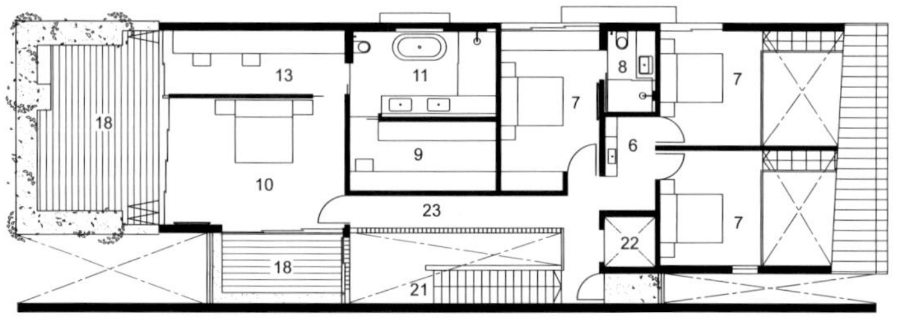

ATTIC

1 FOYER
2 LIVING
3 DINING
4 DRY KITCHEN
5 WET KITCHEN
6 PANTRY
7 BEDROOM
8 BATHROOM
9 WARDROBE
10 MASTER BEDROOM
11 MASTER BATHROOM
12 FAMILY ROOM
13 STUDY
14 WINE CELLAR
15 MUSIC ROOM
16 BIKE STORE
17 STORE
18 TERRACE
19 KOI POND
20 POOL
21 STAIRS
22 LIFT
23 CORRIDOR
24 CAR PORCH
25 LAUNDRY
26 UTILITY
27 HOUSEHOLD SHELTER
28 M&E

A Tale of Two Courts

This house, fortress-like, turns entirely inward on all elevations due to its highly public surroundings. Its long side faces a public footpath while at the rear, a high-rise, high-density public housing development under construction looms. For added privacy, the programmatic organisation was given some tweaks from the typical residential layout. On the first storey, behind the aloofness of an almost-blank façade, serviced spaces such as the wet kitchen and storerooms were moved upfront. They buffer the main living spaces that look inward to a grassy courtyard, anchored lyrically with a sole willow tree.

This is one of two courtyards that shape the house's datum. It separates the common areas from three main bedrooms in the rear. The second courtyard, which the study nooks of these bedrooms look into, is private and introverted compared to the first courtyard. While it is a fully enclosed space, an expansive timber pergola and glass roof above a double-storey atrium gives it a semi-outdoor feel. A good amount of light and wind enter during the day due to side openings between the two roof elements and a high-velocity fan.

The enfilade of spaces through the deep plan lends to long sightlines. It also encourages an easy, fluid navigation of the plan. Placing the main spaces on the first storey, and the entertainment and ancillary programs upstairs protects the former from curious passers-by. The use of sand-coloured face brick to clad the entire house intensifies the monolithic form, while timber-formed concrete ceilings inside enhance the textural palette and sense of nature.

Project Name
— A Tale of Two Courts
Type
— New build of two-storey corner terrace house with an attic
Location
— Wan Tho Avenue, Singapore
Completed
— 2017
Built area
— 794m^2
Site area
— 633m^2
Project team members
— Han Loke Kwang
— 'Ann' Tipnipa Pantipjatuporn
Structural Engineer
— GCE Consulting Engineers
Main Contractor
— Emma Groups Construction Pte Ltd
Photography
— Derek Swalwell

37

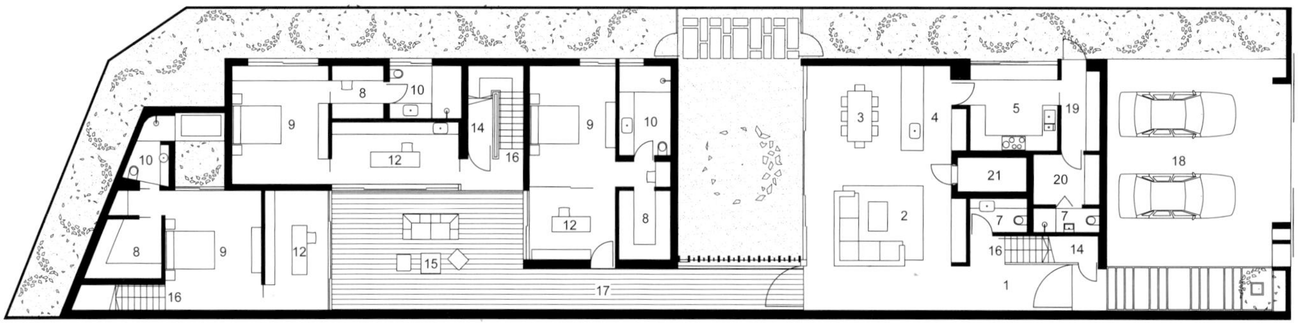

1ST STOREY

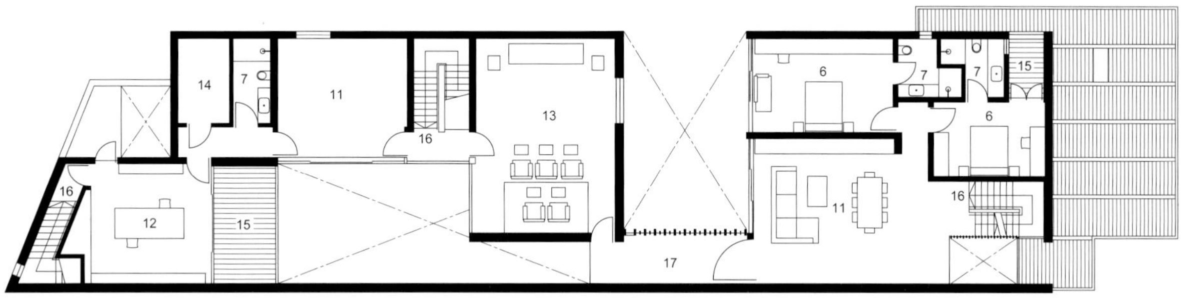

2ND STOREY

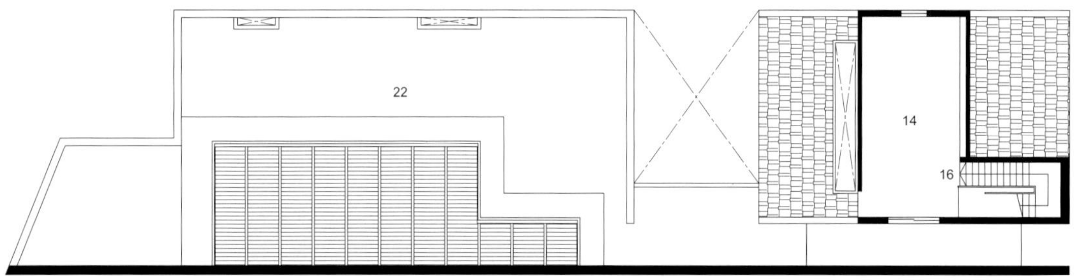

ATTIC

1 FOYER
2 LIVING
3 DINING
4 DRY KITCHEN
5 WET KITCHEN
6 BEDROOM
7 BATHROOM
8 WARDROBE
9 MASTER BEDROOM
10 MASTER BATHROOM
11 FAMILY ROOM
12 STUDY
13 ENTERTAINMENT ROOM
14 STORE
15 TERRACE
16 STAIRS
17 CORRIDOR
18 CAR PORCH
19 LAUNDRY
20 UTILITY
21 HOUSEHOLD SHELTER
22 M&E

Verdant Verandah

— The main screening element of this corner semi-detached house takes the form of a band of concrete brise-soleil that wraps the upper levels. Its design extends beyond that of a screen for privacy and sun-protection. As Han describes, it also aims to capture and intensify nature along the house's perimeter with a series of lush, landscaped verandas immediately adjacent to the indoor spaces.

Plants incorporated into the depth of the concrete shell allow for greenery to layer over as time goes by. It is like an expanding green curtain buffering the liminal spaces that softens the béton brut. The concrete shell gives to every room on the upper levels its own private garden, each with a slightly different character. One has a bathtub set into the veranda, placed literally outside the main body of the house, yet sheltered from the elements and hidden from the street by the screen and greenery.

To prevent monotony, modules were removed at intervals within the basic grid. The result is an architecture defined by asymmetry and syncopation. Offsetting the planar elements in the screen slightly inward enhances the shell's sense of depth in the elevations. A contrasting skin of timber screens wraps the rest of the house. Its lightweight appearance contrasts with the concrete screen's robustness. This juxtaposition creates an architecture of clarity and duality that visually engages while introducing diverse lighting effects in the interior.

Project Name
— Verdant Verandah
Type
— New build of two-storey semi-detached house with an attic, a basement and a swimming pool
Location
— Princess Of Wales Road, Singapore
Completed
— 2018
Built area
— 549m^2
Site area
— 320m^2
Project team members
— Han Loke Kwang
— 'Ann' Tipnipa Pantipjatuporn
— Tran Thi Thu Trang
Structural Engineer
— GCE Consulting Engineers
Main Contractor
— Praxis Contractors Pte Ltd
Photography
— Derek Swalwell

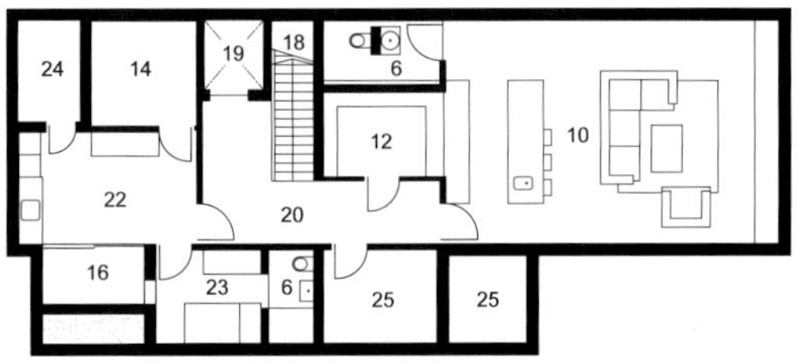

BASEMENT

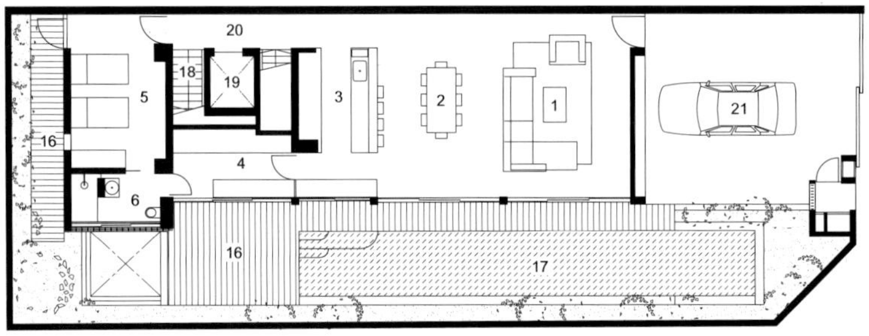

1ST STOREY

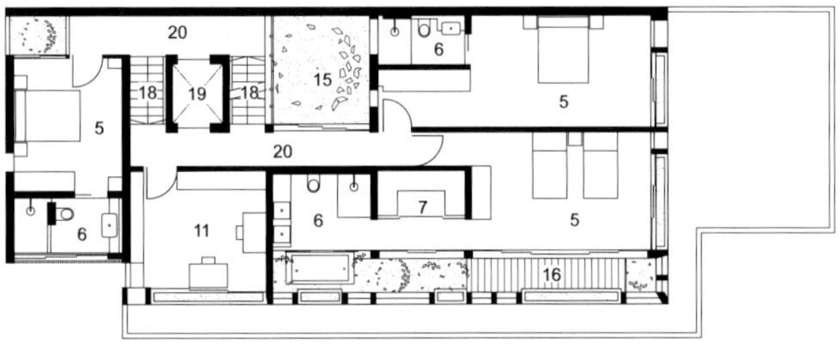

2ND STOREY

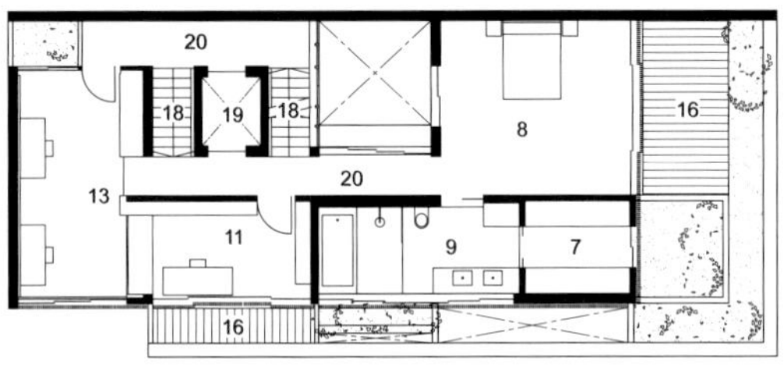

ATTIC

1 LIVING
2 DINING
3 DRY KITCHEN
4 WET KITCHEN
5 BEDROOM
6 BATHROOM
7 WARDROBE
8 MASTER BEDROOM
9 MASTER BATHROOM
10 FAMILY ROOM
11 STUDY
12 WINE CELLAR
13 MUSIC ROOM
14 STORE
15 COURTYARD
16 TERRACE
17 POOL
18 STAIRS
19 LIFT
20 CORRIDOR
21 CAR PORCH
22 LAUNDRY
23 UTILITY
24 HOUSEHOLD SHELTER
25 M&E

Pool House

—— The parti of this detached house reads as a composition of three boxes – two stacked above one another, abutting a third. The latter extrudes along the length of the plot to envelop a twenty-metre-long swimming pool, which was a requisite of the client. Similar to the Room Without Roof project, a house whose pool is internalised by a structural envelope, a concrete portal frames the water body to shape a 'pool house'. A ceiling of aluminium screens that turn down the portal's side varies heat and light intensity in the pool, as well as the adjacent spaces.

On the first storey, the living, dining and dry kitchen are given double volumes to match the height of the pool area. One space extends into the other, blurring interior and exterior. The verticality of the living area is mirrored with a timber staircase whose components appear to float above the dry kitchen. The sculptural form begins as cantilevered steps that segue into the mezzanine. The layered elevations of the mezzanine and the subsequent staircase landing are rendered as lightweight elements, with timber strips sandwiched together in a jaunty pattern.

The informal, open character of the mezzanine corresponds to its programs. At one end is an outdoor terrace that connects with the street while the gym caps the other end. The swimming pool's placement in between combines the workout zones into a continuous trajectory. A pleasant view of water accompanies gym sessions beneath the symbolically energising rust-red tone of the aluminium canopy.

Project Name
—— Pool House
Type
—— New build of two-storey detached house with an attic and a swimming pool
Location
—— Lorong G Telok Kurau, Singapore
Completed
—— 2021
Built area
—— 697m²
Site area
—— 616m²
Project team members
—— Han Loke Kwang
—— Tran Thi Thu Trang
—— Constans Tan
Structural Engineer
—— GCE Consulting Engineers
Main Contractor
—— Emma Groups Construction Pte Ltd
Photography
—— Derek Swalwell

SFS6866H

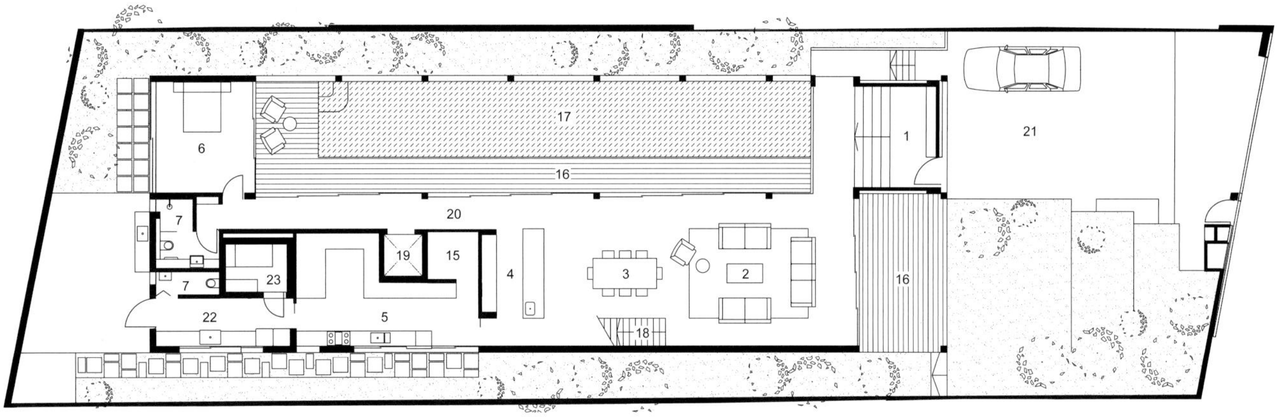

1ST STOREY

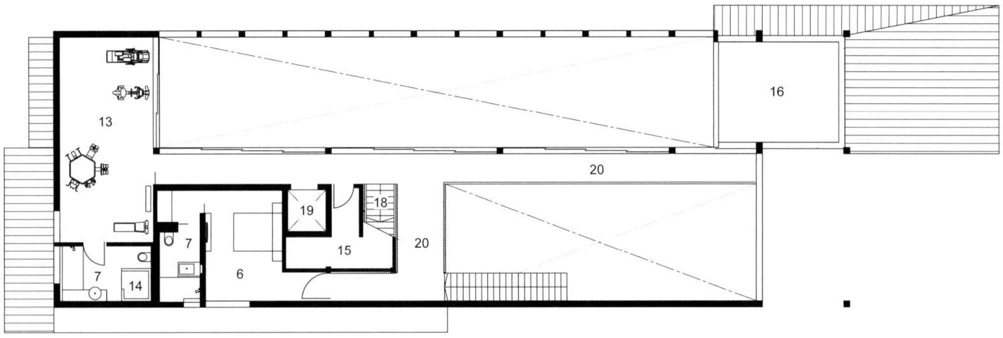

2ND STOREY

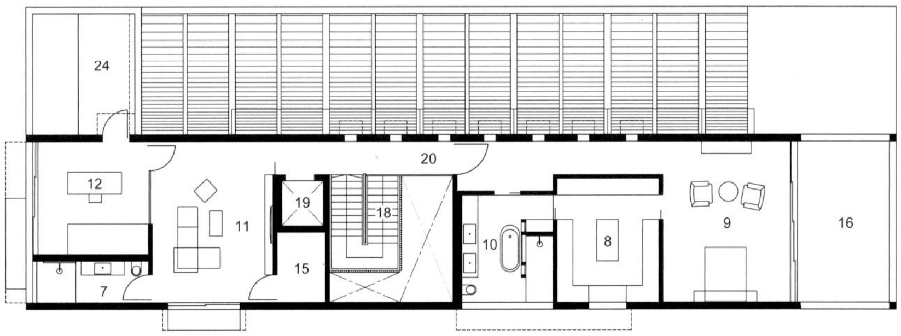

3RD STOREY

1 FOYER
2 LIVING
3 DINING
4 DRY KITCHEN
5 WET KITCHEN
6 BEDROOM
7 BATHROOM
8 WARDROBE
9 MASTER BEDROOM
10 MASTER BATHROOM
11 FAMILY ROOM
12 STUDY
13 GYM
14 SAUNA
15 STORE
16 TERRACE
17 POOL
18 STAIRS
19 LIFT
20 CORRIDOR
21 CAR PORCH
22 LAUNDRY
23 HOUSEHOLD SHELTER
24 M&E

32

Fade to Green

— Taking its cue from the verdant surroundings of the nearby Singapore Botanic Gardens – a UNESCO World Heritage Site – the narrative of nature and its relationship with the dwelling became the key theme in this house. The architecture was inspired by Southeast Asian vernacular houses using tin roofs and timber that were allowed to weather, with parts insouciantly overtaken by planting.

The house presents a similar way of merging building and nature, letting time make its mark on the shell so that nothing is too precious or pristine. As Han describes, contrary to resisting the elements of nature, this house pursues the idea that when the building stops, nature takes over. A timber screen encapsulates the entire top levels of the house. Timber from Norway using Kebony® technology was chosen as it ages well, fading to a chalky grey over time. It is also treated to have all moisture removed to prevent warping. Exposed steel frames and bolts exhibit an industrial nature.

The integral fusing of the architectural skin with landscaping grounds the internal experience, regulated by the detailing of the screen. The timber battens are denser at elevations facing the unbearable western sun in the afternoon and more porous where it turns to the more forgiving morning sun. This density also matches the demands for privacy and diminishes toward the top to let plants flourish. The house is not only green in design and spirit but also in operation, with a rainwater harvester, roof ventilator, solar panels and heat-resistant glazing, making it a worthy case study of holistic sustainable design.

Project Name
— Fade to Green
Type
— New build of two-storey semi-detached house with an attic
Location
— Jalan Harom Setangkai, Singapore
Completed
— 2018
Built area
— 406m^2
Site area
— 293m^2
Project team members
— Han Loke Kwang
— Chong Wen Jin
Structural Engineer
— GCE Consulting Engineers
Main Contractor
— Emma Groups Construction Pte Ltd
Photography
— Derek Swalwell

32

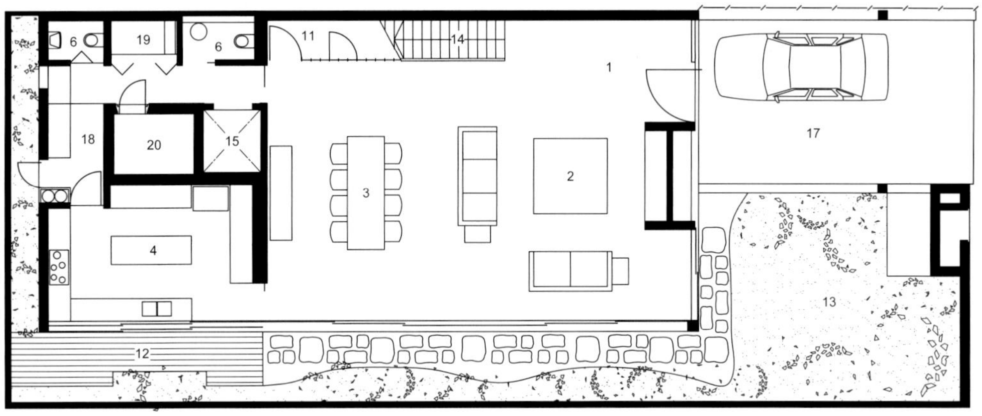

1ST STOREY

2ND STOREY

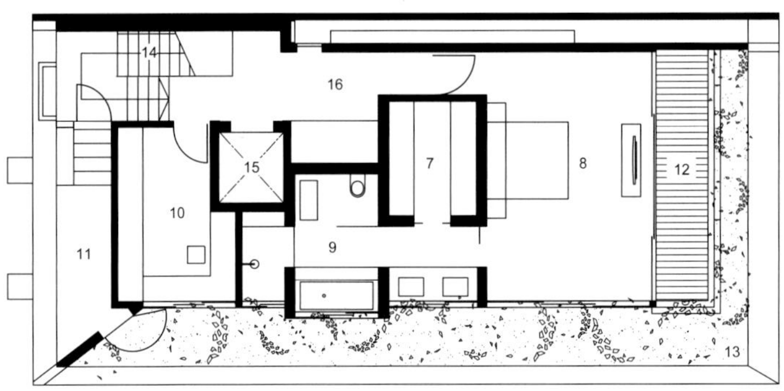

ATTIC

1 FOYER
2 LIVING
3 DINING
4 KITCHEN
5 BEDROOM
6 BATHROOM
7 WARDROBE
8 MASTER BEDROOM
9 MASTER BATHROOM
10 STUDY
11 STORE
12 TERRACE
13 GARDEN
14 STAIRS
15 LIFT
16 CORRIDOR
17 CAR PORCH
18 LAUNDRY
19 UTILITY
20 HOUSEHOLD SHELTER

Intermediate Stories

— In this house, an intricate screen made from customised modular concrete bricks gives the front elevation a sense of depth while lightening the building's strict orthogonal form. On the inside, small ledges lend this surface a more unusual use as a climbing wall for the owner's cats. The screen covers the upper levels of the house where the main spaces are. On the second storey, it fronts a terrace and living room, both of which have lofty double-volume heights to augment the interior-exterior relationship. On a mezzanine, the children's bedrooms overlook this space, resulting in an interactive section.

This sectional layering comes about from the firm's modulation of the terrace house typology based on the envelope control guideline for landed houses in Singapore, released in 2015 by the Urban Redevelopment Authority (URA). Without the need to adhere to mandatory maximum level heights as long as the overall height keeps within the permissible envelope, the house's stratification enjoys greater autonomy and flexibility. The firm was able to accommodate four storeys in a two-and-a-half-storey zone.

As the first storey sits slightly below the existing road line, the car porch and serviced spaces were tucked here. Elevating the living and dining areas bestow them with a more captivating view of the internal terrace instead of the car porch. The concrete screen, off-form concrete surfaces, grey face brick walls and timber components shape a simple, natural foil. A cantilevering staircase, with treads and risers of concrete cast in-situ, and a steel base for banisters, encapsulates this raw materiality in miniature.

Project Name
— Intermediate Stories
Type
— New build of two-storey corner intermediate terrace house with an attic
Location
— Lily Avenue, Singapore
Completed
— 2017
Built area
— 353m^2
Site area
— 196m^2
Project team members
— Han Loke Kwang
— Tran Thi Thu Trang
— Amanda Tay
Structural Engineer
— GCE Consulting Engineers
Main Contractor
— V-Tech Construction Pte Ltd
Photography
— Derek Swalwell

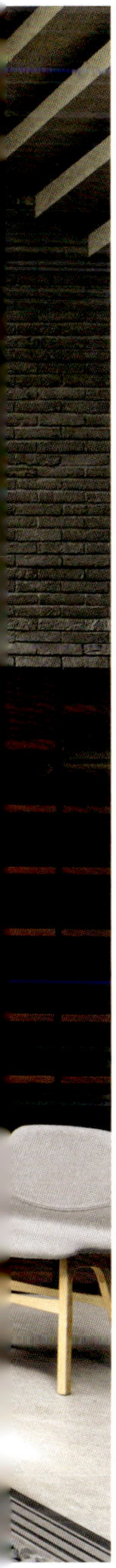

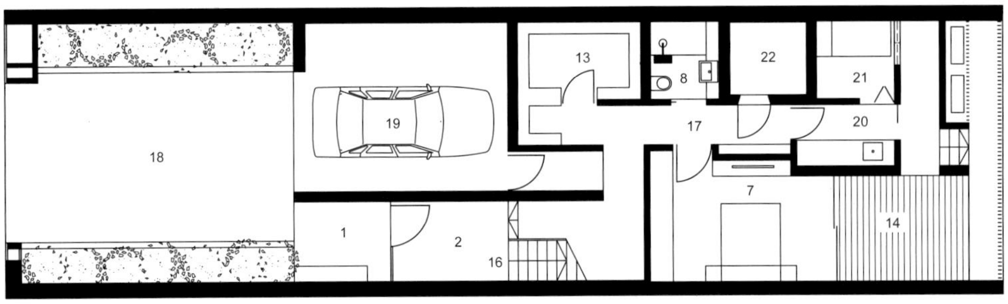

1ST STOREY

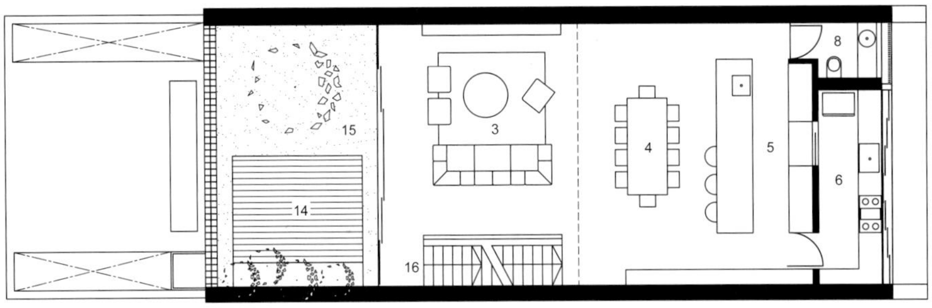

MEZZANINE

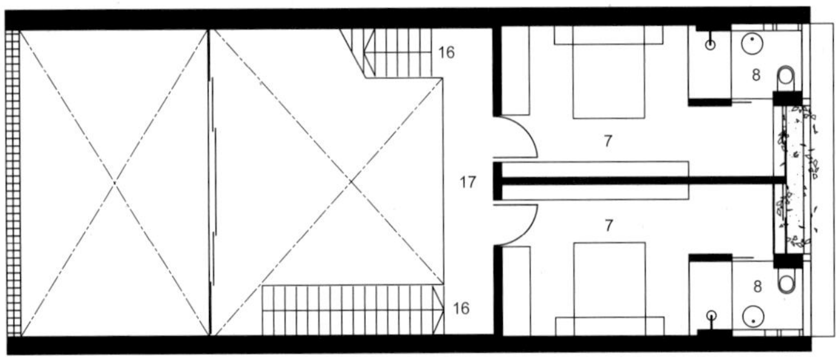

2ND STOREY

ATTIC

1 ENTRANCE
2 FOYER
3 LIVING
4 DINING
5 DRY KITCHEN
6 WET KITCHEN
7 BEDROOM
8 BATHROOM
9 WARDROBE
10 MASTER BEDROOM
11 MASTER BATHROOM
12 STUDY
13 WINE CELLAR
14 TERRACE
15 COURTYARD
16 STAIRS
17 CORRIDOR
18 DRIVEWAY
19 CAR PORCH
20 LAUNDRY
21 UTILITY
22 HOUSEHOLD SHELTER

Viridis Terra

—— This house is one in a row of homes located in a noisy and bustling commercial district. Its rear faces a church, while the front looks to several large retail and medical facilities. Christened Viridis Terra ('green land' in Danish), the architectural intent is to infiltrate the house with greenery and the sense of relief that comes with it where there is none surrounding the plot. The merits of the architecture are also in its employment of passive strategies as much as possible to minimise energy consumption.

A tall, solid brick façade rises up the front of the house to block out the cacophonous sounds and sights of its context. As an additional buffer for the private spaces, the serviced areas are located upfront in the plan. Courtyards introduced on every level, and carefully placed openings and skylights, allow the interior to remain well lit during the day to reduce reliance on artificial illumination. Large apertures between rooms and voids separating the party wall from the spaces improve the home's permeability. While air-conditioning and solar panels are provided, the breathing architecture ensures that the inhabitants remain comfortable enough with just the fans switched on.

Internal and semi-outdoor spaces placed side-by-side in the plan overlook one another in section to create a home where nature expands and flows seamlessly alongside everyday happenings. At the heart of the home, a three-storey courtyard rises up toward a concrete pergola and glass roof, throwing dramatic light and shadow theatrics upon expansive walls.

Project Name
—— Viridis Terra
Type
—— New build of three-storey intermediate terrace house with a mezzanine and an attic
Location
—— Novena Terrace, Singapore
Completed
—— 2020
Built area
—— 532m²
Site area
—— 218m²
Project team members
—— Han Loke Kwang
—— Tiffany Ow
—— Tan Tiong Li
—— Jacelyn Pau
Structural Engineer
—— GCE Consulting Engineers
Main Contractor
—— Toh Kum Swee Pte Ltd
Photography
—— Daniel Koh

31

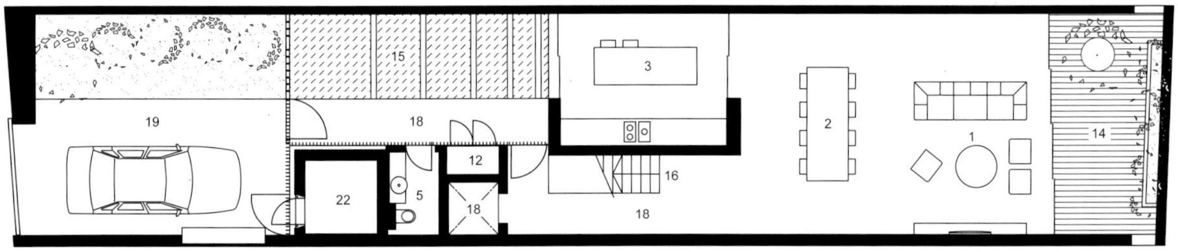

1ST STOREY

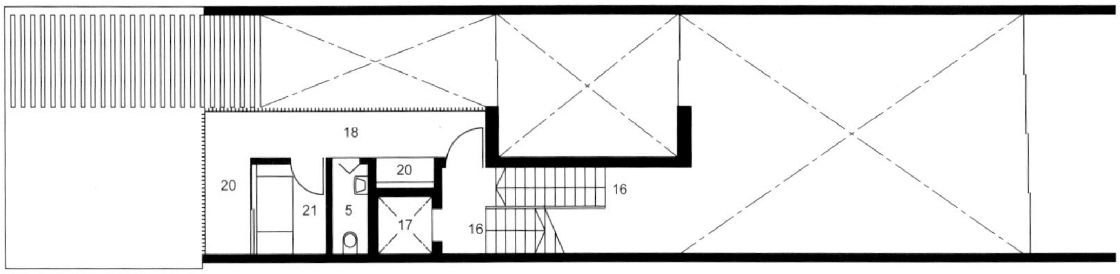

MEZZANINE

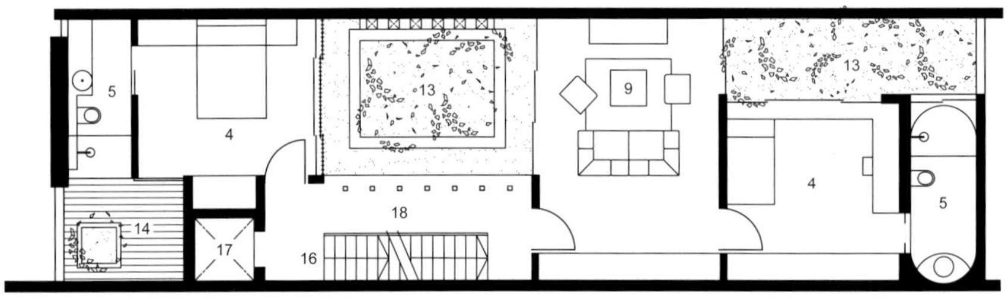

2ND STOREY

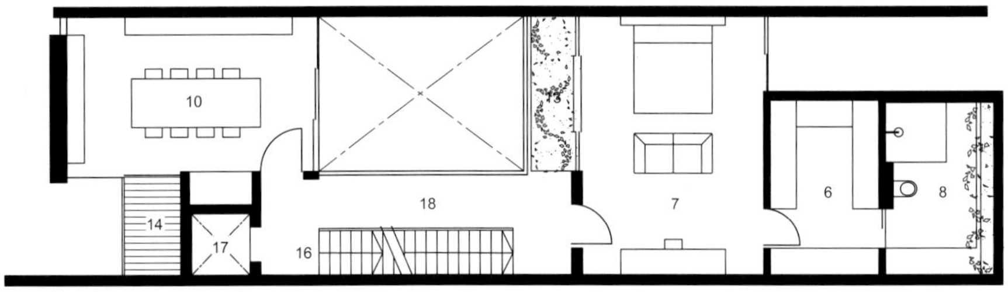

3RD STOREY

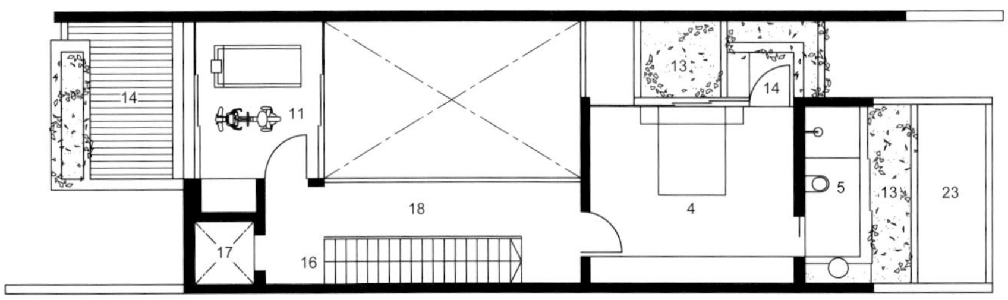

ATTIC

1 LIVING
2 DINING
3 KITCHEN
4 BEDROOM
5 BATHROOM
6 WARDROBE
7 MASTER BEDROOM
8 MASTER BATHROOM
9 FAMILY ROOM
10 STUDY
11 GYM
12 STORE
13 COURTYARD
14 TERRACE
15 WATER FEATURE
16 STAIRS
17 LIFT
18 CORRIDOR
19 CAR PORCH
20 LAUNDRY
21 UTILITY
22 HOUSEHOLD SHELTER
23 M&E

Intervening Light

— Depending on the intervention, light in the tropics can be either a friend or foe. This intermediate terrace house was modulated to enable the former, with light harnessed to uplift the interiors and create a sense of airiness during the day. The main device employed is a plane of horizontal aluminium screens shielding the front elevation from the western sun. The density of the components correlates to the interior needs for privacy and sun shading.

The interior was organised to offer a balance of privacy and connectivity. This was important for the multi-generational family spanning four generations. A mezzanine was added to create four levels in total. Each is given to a generation, from the oldest at the base to the youngest at the top. Despite this clear segregation, the house feels well connected due to overlapping double-volume spaces and courtyards. On the first storey, a voluminous living and dining area doubles as a gallery for the owner's collection of antique Straits Chinese furniture, while the two top levels are bound by a tall, luxuriant courtyard. Terraces at both ends invite lounging in the semi-outdoors.

Another element that enhances the light and sense of lightness within the home is the staircase. It is located at the front of the house for each member to access their respective areas without disturbing the rest of the family. Each staircase tread, made from five pieces of timber supported by a steel section, cantilevers from the wall. The result is a contraption with a floating effect, and whose horizontality makes it appear at one with the front facade.

Project Name
— Intervening Light
Type
— New build of two-storey intermediate terrace house with an attic
Location
— Sunset Way, Singapore
Completed
— 2019
Built area
— 477m^2
Site area
— 285m^2
Project team members
— Han Loke Kwang
— Tiffany Ow
— Diana Yong
— Yao Tian
Structural Engineer
— GCE Consulting Engineers
Main Contractor
— Praxis Contractors Pte Ltd
Photography
— Daniel Koh

98

96 Sunset Way

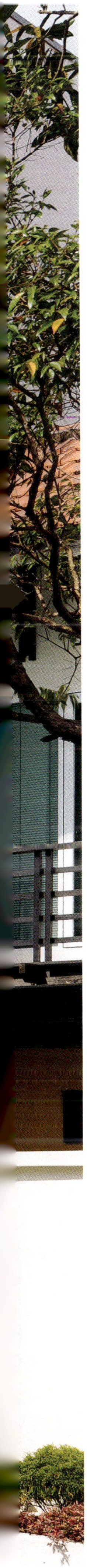

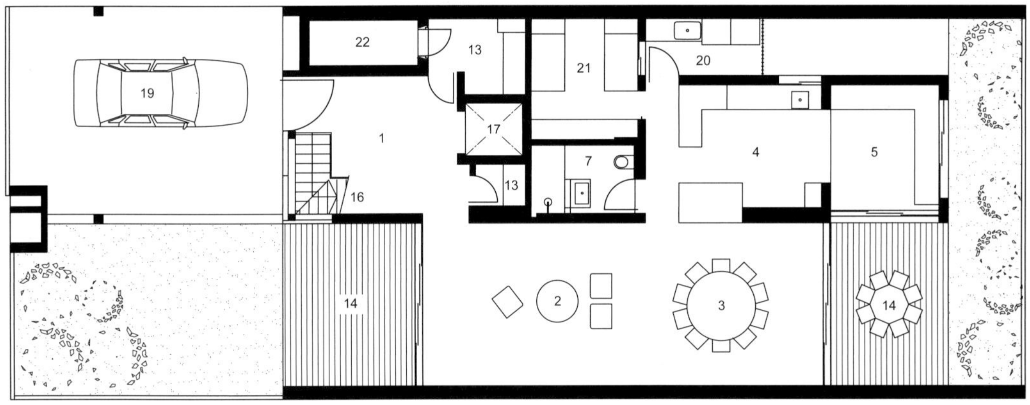

1ST STOREY

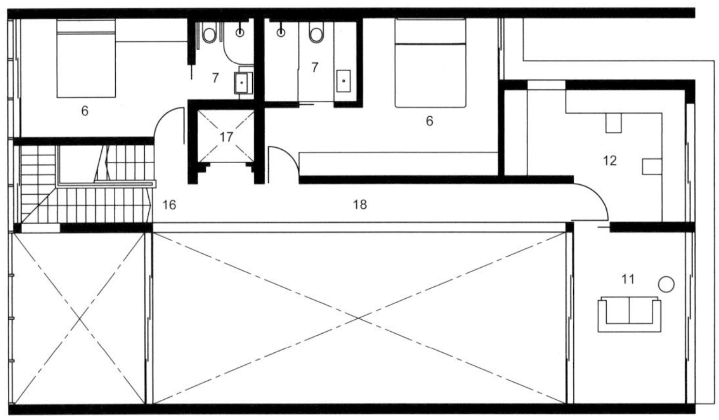

MEZZANINE

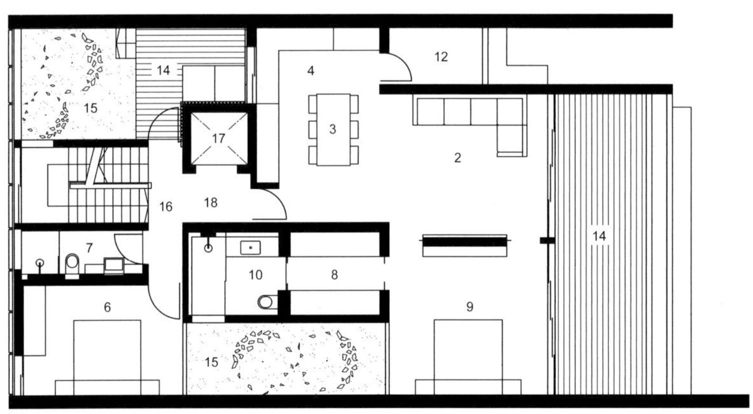

2ND STOREY

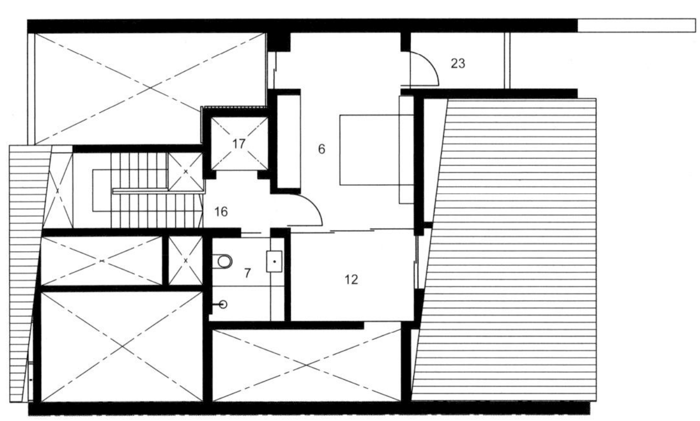

ATTIC

1 FOYER
2 LIVING
3 DINING
4 DRY KITCHEN
5 WET KITCHEN
6 BEDROOM
7 BATHROOM
8 WARDROBE
9 MASTER BEDROOM
10 MASTER BATHROOM
11 FAMILY ROOM
12 STUDY
13 STORE
14 TERRACE
15 COURTYARD
16 STAIRS
17 LIFT
18 CORRIDOR
19 CAR PORCH
20 LAUNDRY
21 UTILITIES
22 HOUSEHOLD SHELTER
23 M&E

The Sculpted Space

Architecture is housed under the canon of art as the highest order of creation. This house, which belongs to an art collector, expresses this literally, with key architectural elements conceived as pieces of art through bold, vigorous and expressive form making. The entire house pays homage to art – its making, exhibition and spirit.

Instead of a white-walled gallery, the main body of the house is a solid off-form concrete volume. This minimises maintenance while still being timeless. At the pool, it morphs into a trellis for sun shading and ventilation to the internal parts. This concrete screen enclosure is itself a gallery, with light and shadow play as nature's mutable artwork. The main living spaces are organised around the pool, which offers a source of calm to everyday activities.

The concrete trellis extends toward the front elevation as part of an asymmetrical, layered composition of forms that includes timber-clad balconies and a totemic sculpture of patinated brass. The latter encases a spiral staircase that floats at the edge of the pool. It vertically connects spaces of art on different levels: The Foyer, The Lounge, The Gallery and The Sculpture Garden at the attic veranda. In The Gallery, a barrel vault ceiling is itself a veritable sculpture. Deeper in the plan is another architectural art piece – a staircase wrapped in timber veneer and whose walls double as surfaces for art. A sense of warmth and visual delight is brought into the home through its staggered shelves and slanted supports under the staircase treads.

Project Name
— The Sculpted Space
Type
— New build of two-storey detached house with a basement, an attic and a swimming pool
Location
— Dunbar Walk, Singapore
Completed
— 2020
Built area
— 623m^2
Site area
— 497m^2
Project team members
— Han Loke Kwang
— Tran Thi Thu Trang
— Tan Tiong Li
Structural Engineer
— GCE Consulting Engineers
Main Contractor
— Emma Groups Construction Pte Ltd
Photography
— Daniel Koh

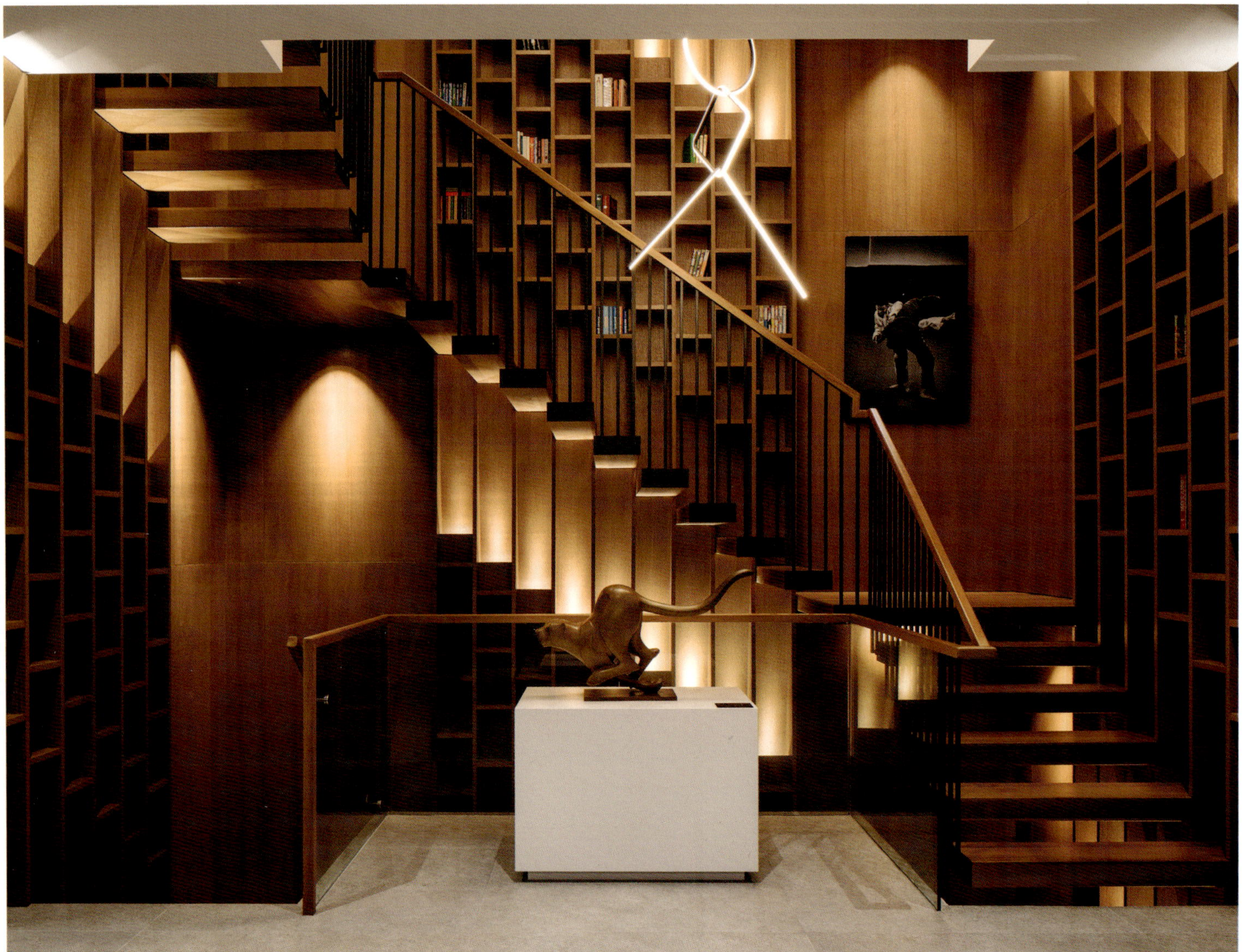

BASEMENT

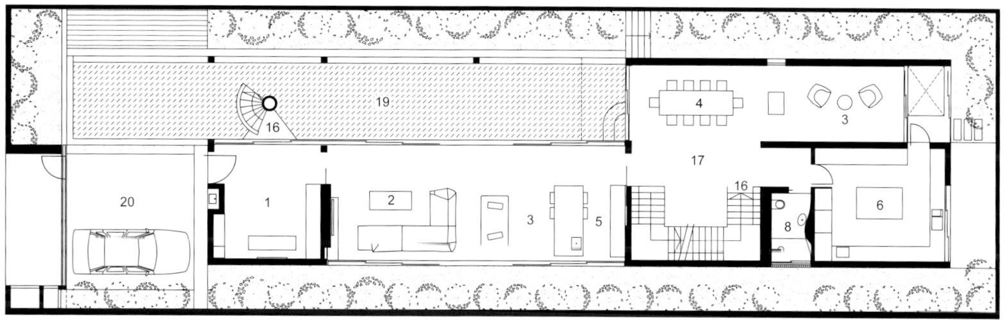

1ST STOREY

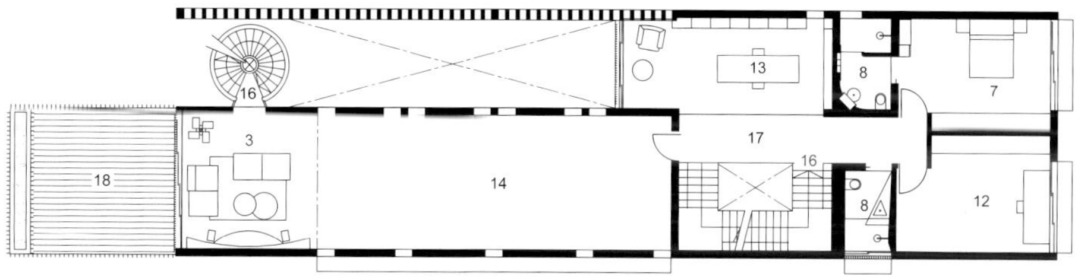

2ND STOREY

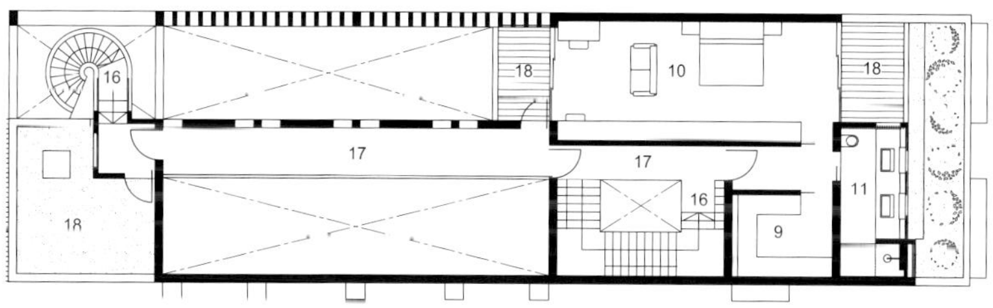

3RD STOREY

1 FOYER
2 LIVING
3 LOUNGE
4 DINING
5 DRY KITCHEN
6 WET KITCHEN
7 BEDROOM
8 BATHROOM
9 WARDROBE
10 MASTER BEDROOM
11 MASTER BATHROOM
12 FAMILY ROOM
13 STUDY
14 ART GALLERY
15 STORE
16 STAIRS
17 CORRIDOR
18 TERRACE
19 POOL
20 CAR PORCH
21 LAUNDRY
22 UTILITY
23 HOUSEHOLD SHELTER
24 M&E

Green Revelation

— Upon approaching this house, one is presented with a vision of resplendent greenery, starting from a lushly planted boundary wall, then a verdant ground storey garden, and finally, luxuriant landscaping on the rooftop. This green view is a prelude to the abundance of nature woven into the architecture, comprising six separate gardens and courtyards spread across various levels. It culminates at the rear of the house with a densely planted courtyard that buffers the interiors from the neighbour sitting on higher land, while letting natural light and ventilation into the home through gaps in the concrete framework and brick infill walls.

This palette is deployed to the rest of the house, giving it an unassuming and natural character. The staircase is poised alongside this courtyard such that vertical movement through the house is perennially rewarded with scenes of changing light, accompanied by the sway of leaves, and a sense of life and growth. On the first storey, the double-volume living room is shielded from the elements with the courtyard on one side and a deep terrace facing the front garden on the other. Timber cladding this terrace demarcates a portal for the inhabitants to sit and enjoy the view of the garden and koi pond.

On the front elevation, a climatic skin in the form of a sliding aluminium screen filters views and the harshness of the western sun. Compared to the main courtyard that impresses with its luxuriance, the intimate courtyard outside the family room with a grotto offers quietude and calm.

Project Name
— Green Revelation
Type
— New build of three-storey detached house with an attic and a rooftop swimming pool
Location
— Mariam Close, Singapore
Completed
— 2019
Built area
— 650m²
Site area
— 568m²
Project team members
— Han Loke Kwang
— Tiffany Ow
— Diana Yong
— Yao Tian
Structural Engineer
— Thymn Pte Ltd
Main Contractor
— Emma Groups Construction Pte Ltd
Photography
— Masano Kawana

20

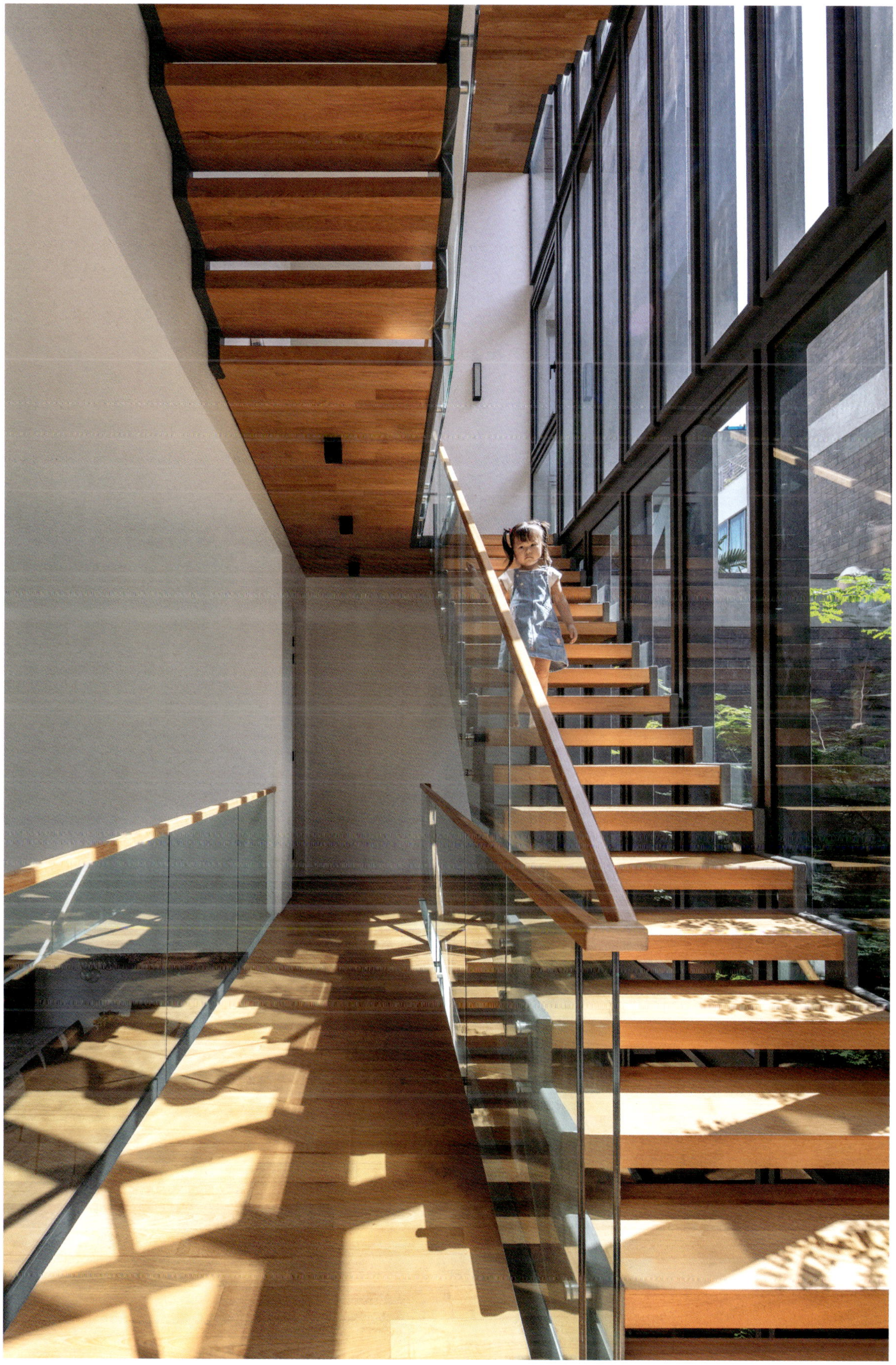

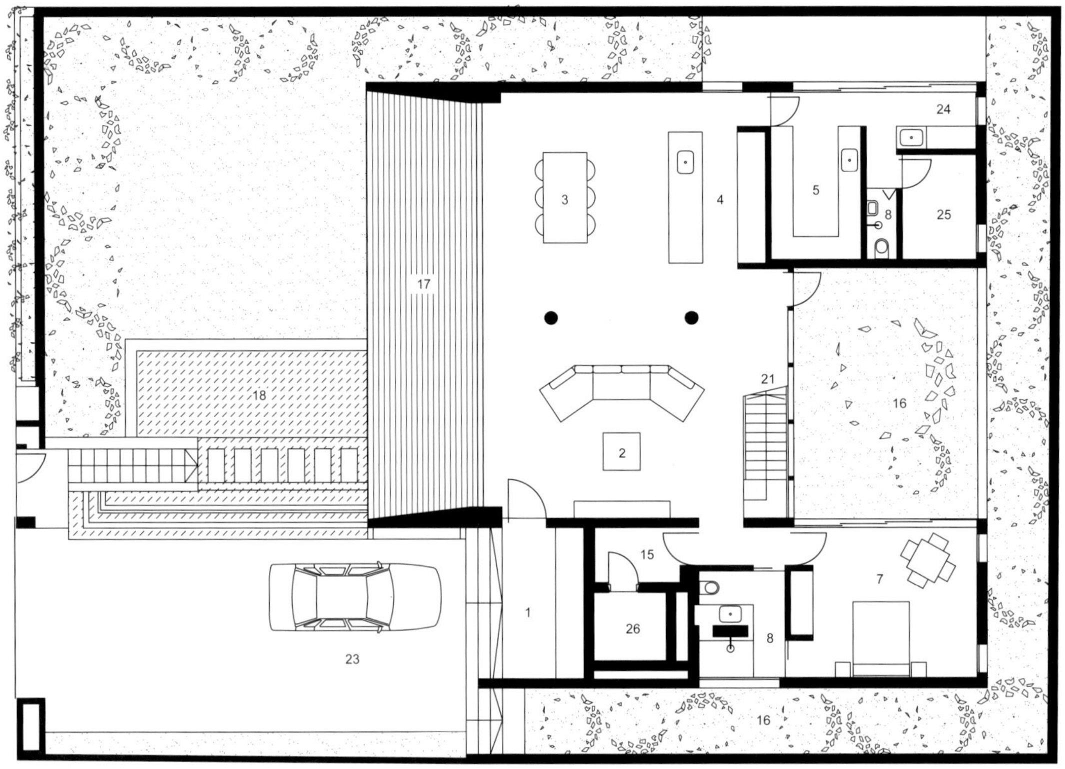

1ST STOREY

1 FOYER
2 LIVING
3 DINING
4 DRY KITCHEN
5 WET KITCHEN
6 PANTRY
7 BEDROOM
8 BATHROOM
9 WARDROBE
10 MASTER BEDROOM
11 MASTER BATHROOM
12 STUDY
13 GYM
14 ENTERTAINMENT ROOM
15 STORE
16 COURTYARD
17 TERRACE
18 KOI POND
19 POOL
20 JACUZZI
21 STAIRS
22 CORRIDOR
23 CAR PORCH
24 LAUNDRY
25 UTILITY
26 HOUSEHOLD SHELTER
27 M&E

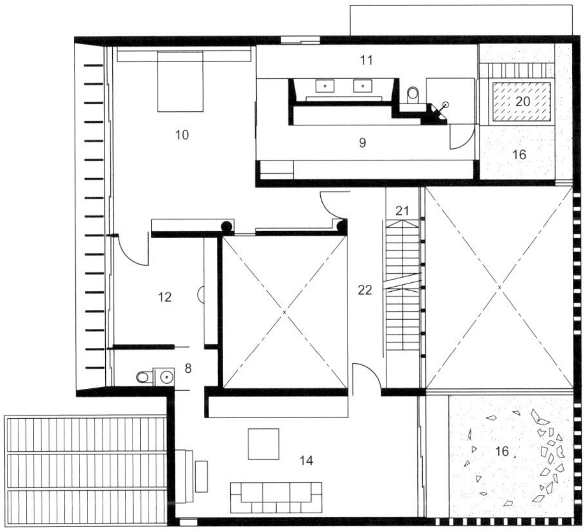

MEZZANINE

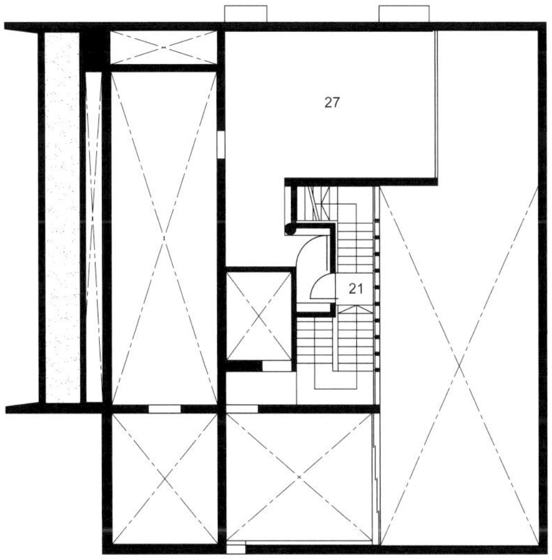

ATTIC

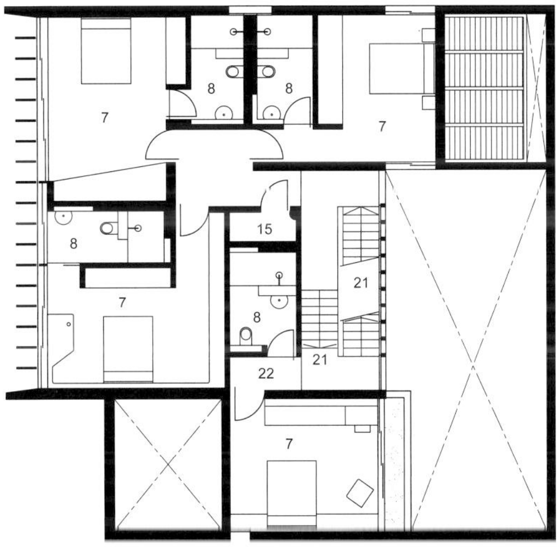

2ND STOREY

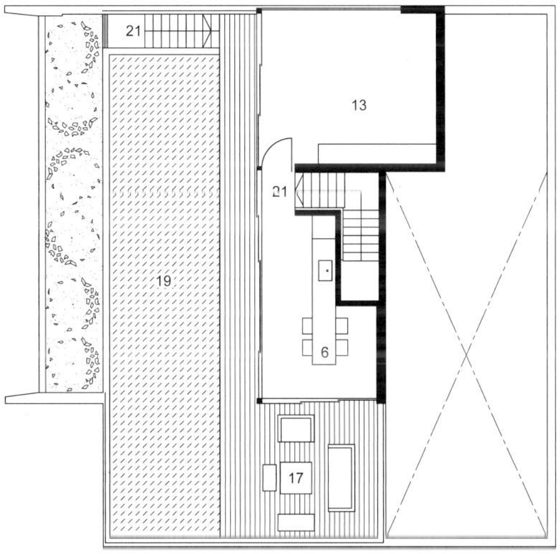

ROOF

Between Us 2

The parti of this project reads as two long blocks tunnelling down the length of the plot. They are divided by a central void with plentiful landscaping, creating a green spine that enlivens the dwellings on all levels. The simple parti directly reflects the program of two detached houses for a pair of siblings and their families. The courtyard offers both segregation and union, while the formal symmetry projects the idea of equality and balance.

Behind the main timber gate, the courtyard is a picture of calm with timber decking from which four trees protrude against a backdrop of lush landscaping. Hidden within this luscious greenery is a large skylight that brightens rooms in the basement. The greenery extends towards the rear in the form of a vertical garden, which steps down into a smaller courtyard adjacent to entertainment spaces. This lower courtyard offers both families a more intimate gathering space.

The architecture has been detailed to contrast lightness and solidarity. Walls of grey stone at the entrance and internally are offset by lightweight elements, such as timber screens, metal framing, and the thin flat roofs of the two main volumes and the car porch canopy. Timber screens give control of views, light and ventilation. The density of the screens correlates with specific needs for privacy. This passive climatic device accompanies formal articulations such as protruding roof eaves to craft a sustainable tropical house.

Project Name
— Between Us 2
Type
— New build of a pair of two-storey detached houses with a basement
Location
— Dunsfold Drive, Singapore
Completed
— 2019
Built area
— 1008m^2
Site area
— 1029m^2
Project team members
— Han Loke Kwang
— Nicholas Gomes
— 'Ann' Tipnipa Pantipjatuporn
Structural Engineer
— GCE Consulting Engineers
Main Contractor
— QS Builders Pte Ltd
Photography
— Masano Kawana

BASEMENT

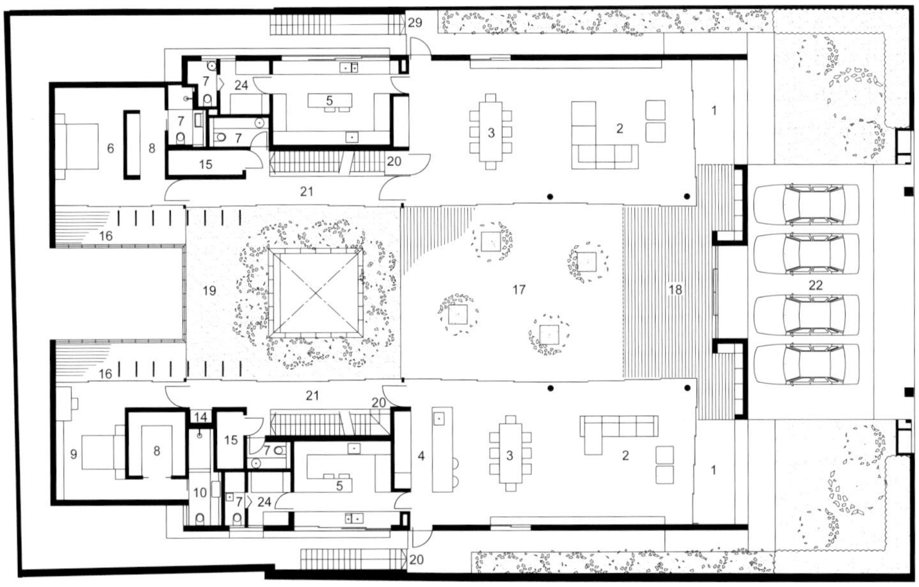

1ST STOREY

1 FOYER
2 LIVING
3 DINING
4 DRY KITCHEN
5 WET KITCHEN
6 BEDROOM
7 BATHROOM
8 WARDROBE
9 MASTER BEDROOM
10 MASTER BATHROOM
11 FAMILY ROOM
12 STUDY
13 ENTERTAINMENT ROOM
14 ALTAR
15 STORE
16 PATIO
17 COURTYARD
18 TERRACE
19 GARDEN
20 STAIRS
21 CORRIDOR
22 CAR PORCH
23 LAUNDRY
24 UTILITY
25 HOUSEHOLD SHELTER

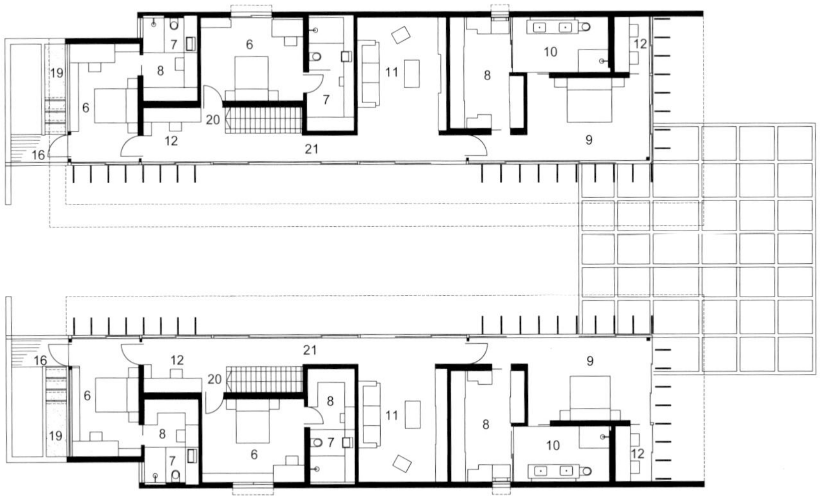

2ND STOREY

Concrete Yin Yang

—— This project features manifold juxtapositions – of form, material, atmosphere, and between nature and shelter. The result of that architectural tension heightens the senses and invokes curiosity. The site conditions inform the exaggerated tectonics. The rear and one long elevation of the detached house looks into neighbouring houses, while the front faces the west and a hard streetscape. The fourth elevation on the other long side has more pleasant views of a field across a road.

A concrete shell wraps the house, its footprint tracing the trapezoidal shape of the land that narrows from front to back. The design of this element, which is largely opaque on the three sides with undesirable views and open on the fourth, makes the project one of the firm's clearest expressions of the dichotomy between a site's positive and negative prospects. At the top of the house, it morphs into a concrete lattice, providing shade to the fourth elevation's glazed skin. The perforations also free the landscaping at the attic's open terrace.

This terrace is one of three lushly landscaped, curvilinear semi-open spaces that are counterpoints to the concrete envelope's precise geometry. The first backdrops the shapely swimming pool on the first storey, joined to a water feature where a bonsai tree stands as an element of surprise behind the car porch's concrete wall. The second extends from the master bedroom and is experienced as a bridge that joins to a large terrace. Creepers drape thickly over its walls, evoking a bucolic retreat in the living room beneath. The abundant greenery throughout the house softens the hardness of glass and concrete, in addition to bringing a sense of calm and comforting shadows to the interior spaces.

Project Name
—— Concrete Yin Yang
Type
—— New build of two-storey detached house with a basement, an attic, and a swimming pool
—— Jalan Langgar Bedok, Singapore
Completed
—— 2022
Built area
—— 556m²
Site area
—— 479m²
Project team members
—— Han Loke Kwang
—— Tiffany Ow
—— Jacelyn Pau
Structural Engineer
—— GCE Consulting Engineers
Main Contractor
—— Emma Groups Construction Pte Ltd
Photography
—— Derek Swalwell

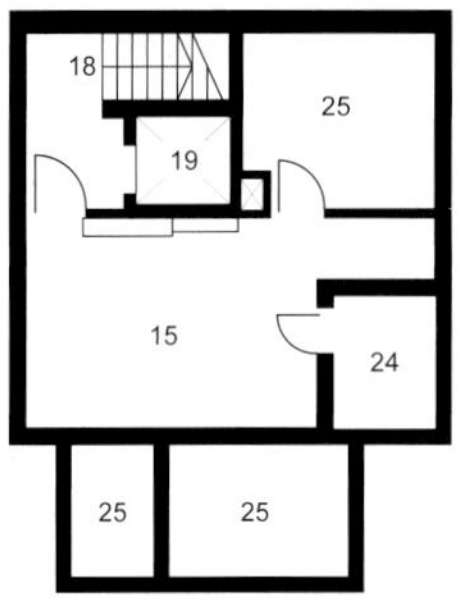

BASEMENT

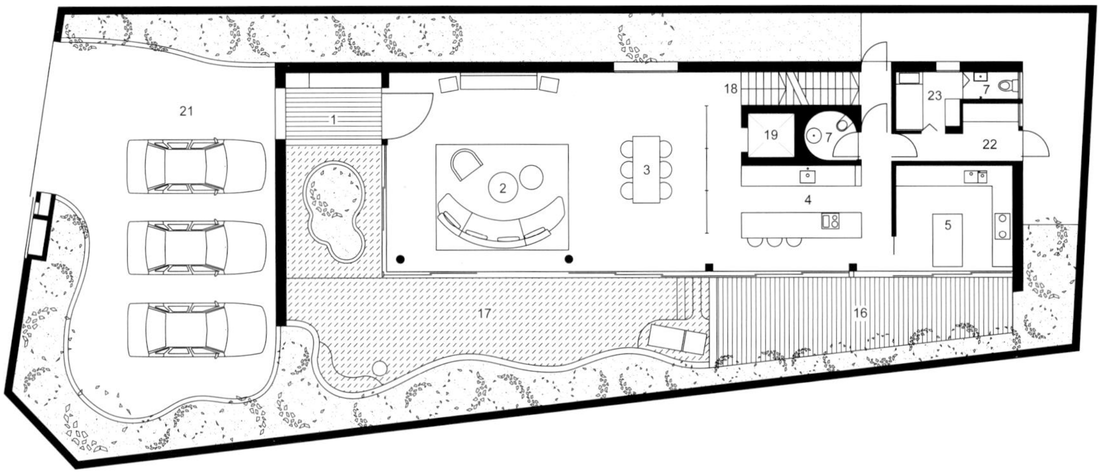

1ST STOREY

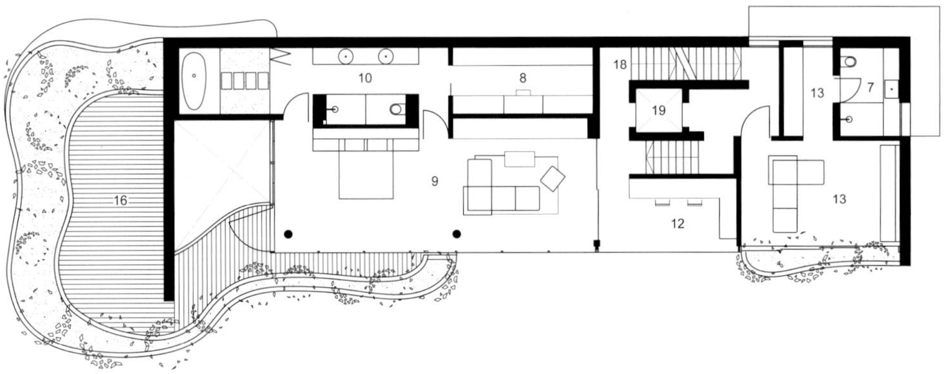

2ND STOREY

1 FOYER
2 LIVING
3 DINING
4 DRY KITCHEN
5 WET KITCHEN
6 BEDROOM
7 BATHROOM
8 WARDROBE
9 MASTER BEDROOM
10 MASTER BATHROOM
11 FAMILY ROOM
12 STUDY
13 AUDIO ROOM/PANTRY
14 GYM
15 STORE
16 TERRACE
17 POOL
18 STAIRS
19 LIFT
20 CORRIDOR
21 CAR PORCH
22 LAUNDRY
23 UTILITY
24 HOUSEHOLD SHELTER
25 M&E

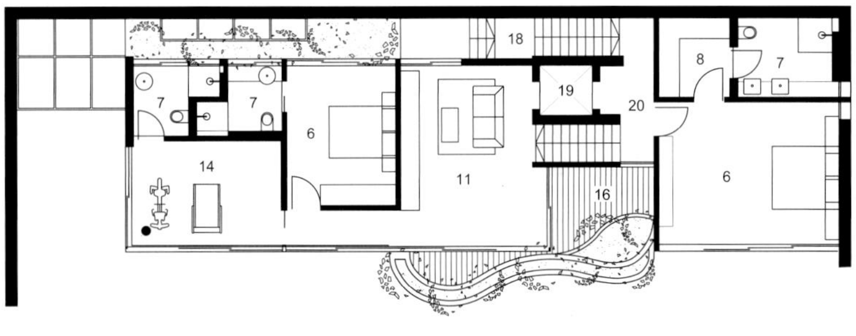

ATTIC

A Black & White Classic

—— Black and White bungalows built in the late 19th century to the pre-war era enjoy conservation status in Singapore due to their heritage. These buildings are a rarity in Singapore and are only available for rent from the Singapore Land Authority. The firm was engaged to work on one such building – an anomaly in the firm's portfolio that comprises mainly new builds. Located in a prime residential district close to shopping facilities, its sprawling bucolic surroundings, lined with matured trees, buffer it from the commercial bustle.

The building was unfortunately gutted in a devastating fire that left nothing except the first storey brick structure. This meant that most of the architectural components, such as the terracotta pitched roofs, French doors and column mouldings, had to be restored. The original layout was reinstated, and finishes selected to retain a sense of history but updated for modern-day living.

While the layout is straightforward – living, dining and dry kitchen on the first storey, and bedrooms upstairs – the spaces are commodious. Included in the scope of works was the basic renovation of two outhouses where the kitchen, laundry and maids' rooms are located, following the original planning of servant and served spaces. On the second storey, a veranda opens up to the view of lush tree canopies. To improve this semi-outdoor space for security, modern comforts and protection against the elements, a frameless vertical window encloses it, so subtly incorporated into the architecture that it dematerialises into the greenery.

Project Name
—— A Black & White Classic
Type
—— Two-storey conservation house
Location
—— Seton Close, Singapore
Completed
—— 2018
Built area
—— 430m^2
Site area
—— 20,017m^2
Project team members
—— Han Loke Kwang
—— Goh Chiou Hwa
—— Tiffany Ow
Structural Engineer
—— SB Ng & Associates C E
Main Contractor
—— Logistics Construction Pte Ltd
Photography
—— Derek Swalwell

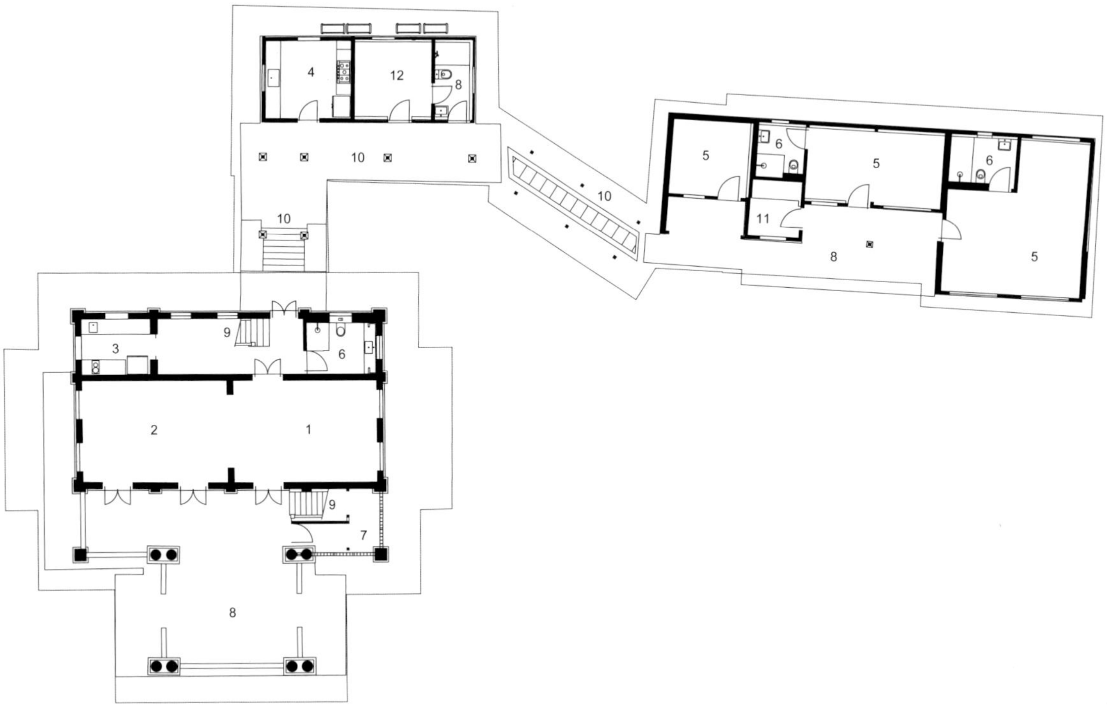

1ST STOREY

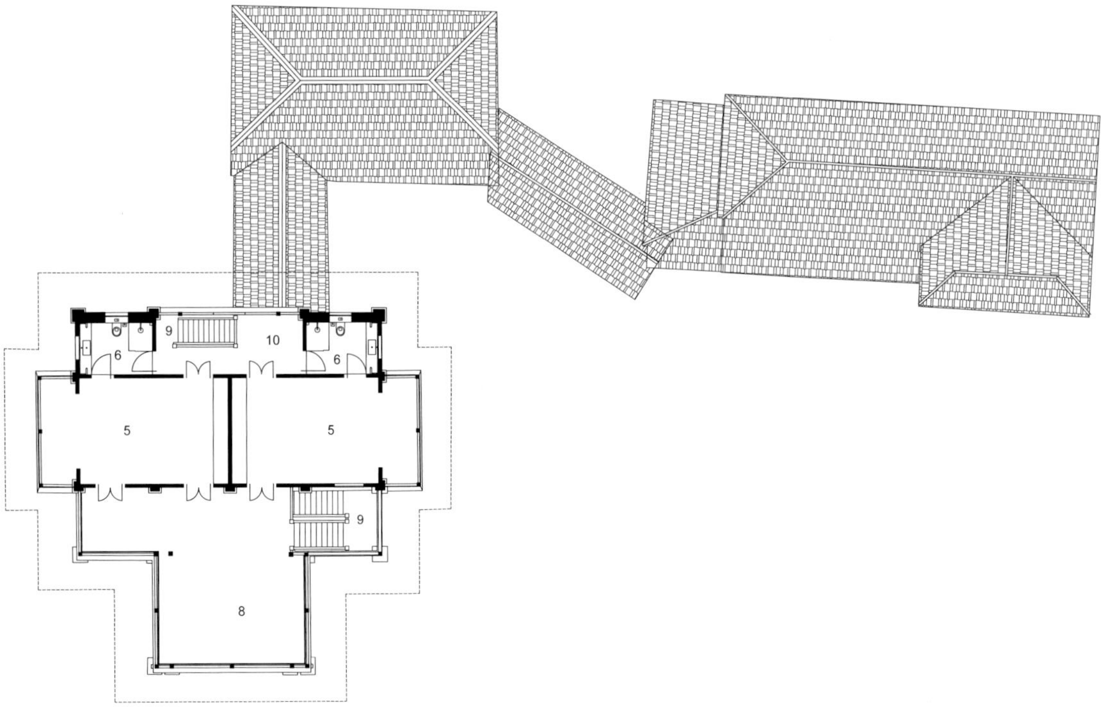

2ND STOREY

1 LIVING
2 DINING
3 DRY KITCHEN
4 WET KITCHEN
5 BEDROOM
6 BATHROOM
7 STORE
8 VERANDA
9 STAIRS
10 LINKWAY
11 LAUNDRY
12 UTILITY

Shophouse Redux

—— Due to gentrification and intensification, most shophouses in Singapore's Central Business District have been converted fully to commercial uses. However as the owners intend to work and live in this particular shophouse located in the Kampong Glam heritage district, the project presented a rare opportunity to tease out the creative potential of the shophouse's original functionality with commercial activity downstairs and dwelling upstairs.

An additional challenge was fitting the programs into a narrow site just 3.6 metres wide. Behind the charcoal-coloured façade and timber fenestrations, the firm's ability to condense function into a tight footprint without sacrificing delight is well exhibited. The ground floor office is partitioned into three sections: the reception and meeting room upfront, the workspace in the middle, and a pantry in the rear where a green wall adds life to the internalised space. Sliding doors between each room allow for expansion or division of space.

The second-storey residence also has three parts within an open plan: a dining area in the rear, a kitchen and bathroom under the bedroom mezzanine linked by a lithe metal spiral staircase, and, lastly, the living area where windows open the home to scenes of urban life. Storage along the length of the shophouse on both levels maintains visual order, while materiality differentiates their programs – a grey and white palette gives the office a sense of formality, and upstairs, a raw aesthetic prevails with the bricks of the party walls exposed. Timber, employed in good amounts on both levels, brings coherence to the two-part scheme.

Project Name
—— Shophouse Redux
Type
—— Two-storey conservation mixed-used shophouse with a mezzanine
Location
—— Jalan Pisang, Singapore
Completed
—— 2016
Built area
—— 146m^2
Site area
—— 80m^2
Project team members
—— Han Loke Kwang
—— Tran Thi Thu Trang
—— Goh Chiou Hwa
Structural Engineer
—— PTS Consultants
Main Contractor
—— Renobest Builders
Photography
—— Derek Swalwell

THE LAB
WATIGA & CO.
WATIGA TRUST
LICENSED TRUST COMPANY
3
WE'RE
OPEN

WATIGA & CO.
WATIGA TRUST

EXIT

EXIT

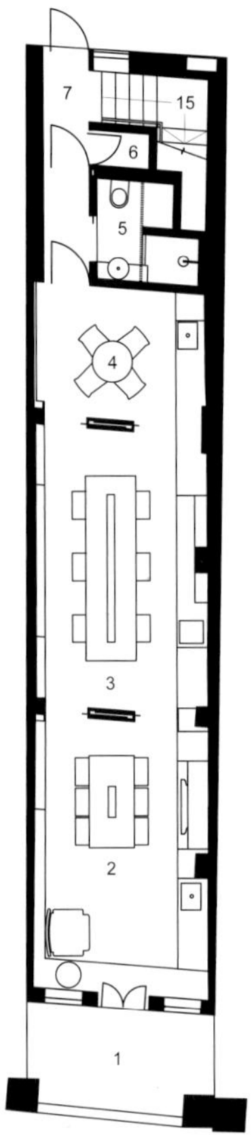

1ST STOREY

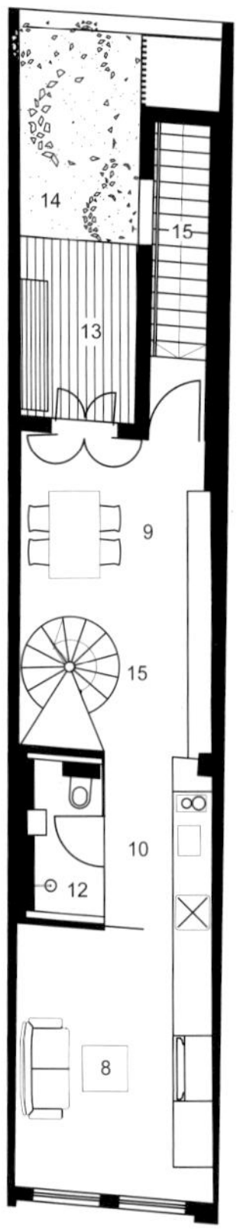

2ND STOREY

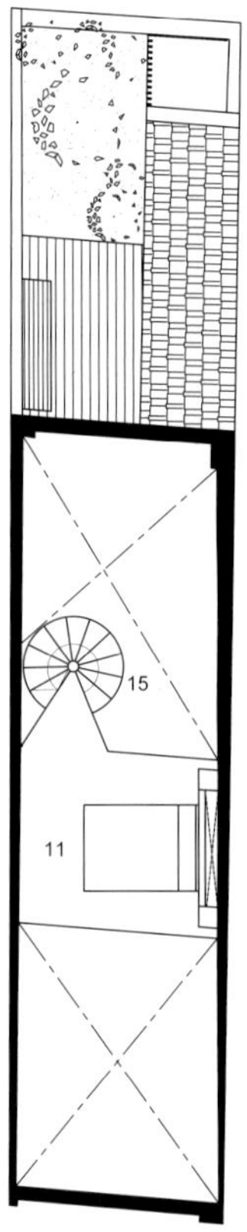

MEZZANINE

1 FIVE-FOOT WAY
2 RECEPTION
3 WORKSPACE
4 PANTRY
5 BATHROOM
6 STORE
7 REAR FOYER
8 LIVING
9 DINING
10 KITCHENETTE
11 MASTER BEDROOM
12 MASTER BATHROOM
13 ROOF TERRACE
14 ROOF GARDEN
15 STAIRS

Company Profile

HYLA Architects was founded in 1994 with a firm belief in design excellence and professional service.

HYLA strives to push the boundaries of modern tropical architecture, continuously seeking to create new typologies that embody the contemporary Asian lifestyle. Values of clarity, simplicity, honesty, and dynamism fuels the firm's ambition to create timeless, unique, and personal works of architecture exemplified through their extensive portfolio of high-end landed homes.

The firm has won numerous accolades, including *The Living Space* INDE Award, Singapore Institute of Architect's *Design Award*, Urban Redevelopment Authority's *Architectural Heritage Award*, and the *Gold Award - Best in Hospitality Design* by the Society of Interior Designers Singapore, among others.

HYLA's work is regularly featured in monographs and magazines internationally, including being selected in the *Phaidon Atlas of 21st Century Architecture* as one of the 1000 exemplary works of architecture around the world.

Scan the QR code to find out more about us.